The Imaginary Networks of Political Power

Roger Bartra

Illustrated by Adela Trueta
Translated by Claire Joysmith

Rutgers University Press
New Brunswick, New Jersey

Library of Congress Cataloging-in-Publication Data

Bartra, Roger.
    [Redes imaginarias del poder político. English]
    The imaginary networks of political power / Roger Bartra ;
illustrated by Adela Trueta ; translated by Claire Joysmith.
      p.   cm.
    Translation of: Las redes imaginarias del poder político.
    Includes bibliographical references and index.
    ISBN 0-8135-1741-9 (cloth).—ISBN 0-8135-1742-7 (pbk.)
    1. Power (Social sciences) I. Title.
JC330.B35313   1992
306.2—dc20   91-23147
                                              CIP

British Cataloging-in-Publication information available

The author gratefully acknowledges translation assistance
provided for this book by the Program for the Support of
Research Projects of the Universidad Nacional Autónoma de
México.

The Imaginary Networks of Political Power

Contents

Preface to the American Edition

This essay is a book of transition; a true rite of passage, in which, as an author, I find the need to cross frontiers and invite the reader to join me on a journey that helps us to understand the end of the millennium. As a remote descendant of Surrealism and as a participant in the cultural upheaval of 1968, there was a time when I ingenuously believed, together with André Breton, that the powers of imagination can never be domesticated, and that in order to change life it is necessary—as the Latin Quarter graffiti proclaimed—for "power to be taken over by the imagination." But the years that followed the May 1968 outburst in Paris proved that the imagination in power would create new forms of political power legitimacy. Thus, not only can imagination be domesticated, but its meek and dim expressions are becoming the most efficient adversaries of libertarian utopias. To understand this situation—now known as *postmodern*—has become a difficult but necessary transition.

With the bitter taste of disenchantment, I decided to embark on the reflection of new forms of mediation, many of which seemed to emerge from the very heart of the utopian dreams my generation valued most. It thus came about that in the mid-seventies I began a series of trips to Europe—including a two-year sojourn in Paris—with the purpose of observing at close range how the so-called structures of political mediation worked. I had already lived in Paris in the proud condition of Third World students who felt they were the messengers of the revolutionary spark and the subversive imagination. In my dual condition as a student and as a Latin American I felt I was part of the long march summoned by Che Guevara and Marcuse, by Ho Chi Minh and Foucault, by Mao and Sartre. A few years later, my old Parisian *rive gauche* teachers seemed like wrecked idols that belonged to an abandoned territory. These frontiers of disenchantment had to be crossed towards an already postmodern exile. Moreover, these revolutionary heroes showed obvious signs of their link with the most degraded forms of socialist authoritarianism.

Now that many of our models were falling apart, how could the critical anatomy of the modern industrial society be undertaken? With the concern of an anthropologist, I experienced intensely the Parisian life of disenchantment, wandered through the streets of divided Berlin, shared the joys of post-Franco Spain and the fears of my friends in Brezhnev's Moscow, and held discussions with British radicals in a pre-Thatcher London. So as not to forget my origins, I made a couple of brief treks to the Third World: I took the way to Kathmandu in search of *another* reality, which I did not find; a stay in Havana rounded off my disillusion; I bathed in the sacred waters of the Ganges, which were flooding Calcutta at the time of my visit, but did not recover my peace of mind; and my brief trips to the Philippines and Panama did little to fortify my exhausted Third-World spirit.

In Europe I planned exercises in participating observation along the purest Malinowskian lines. While I approached the experiences of the French Left, my obsession as an ethnologist gave me no peace: these wild Europeans possessed important secrets, jealously concealed ancient formulas that would explain why the doors of the future were closed. I went along with my questions to knock at Louis Althusser's door in the Rue d'Ulm, questions which he very kindly left unanswered. I also questioned Michel Foucault, went to his lectures at the College de France, and became convinced that structuralism was a wall that came between my doubts and the secrets I wanted to unveil. My research began to shape itself and took on the form of some strange texts which were not entirely approved of among my colleagues in anthropology and sociology even though the social sciences were already beginning to feel the happy influence of Roland Barthes.

Fortunately, a linguist and friend of mine, Daniel Cazés, helped me during that period in my madcap quest; without his guidance, it would have been very difficult to become accustomed to the French life-style, and without the lengthy conversations we had at the Sorbonne and at the Parisian bistros, I would never have been able to decipher so rapidly certain hieroglyphics of the European culture. During that entire period of research I had the support of the Instituto de Investigaciones Sociales of the Universidad Nacional Autónoma de México.

When I concluded my research, I crossed the frontiers once again and returned to my country, bringing with me the results and the secrets I thought I had seized from those wild Europeans. There I eagerly discussed my manuscript with other Mexicans who were also worried by the course of European history. I debated the problems of socialism with Octavio Paz—who read my text before it was published—and I am glad to have been right when I defended the possibility—that began to materialize in 1989—of reforms in authoritarian systems, as opposed to his idea that a new alternative for the USSR and Central Europe could be found only through war. I discussed with writer Carlos Monsiváis and philosopher Luis Villoro the problems of the manipulation of marginality and minority groups: the topic remains a heated one. I wish to thank all three of them heartily for their comments and for the new lines of reflection they suggested.

My manuscript has now embarked on a new journey, this time across the frontier to the United States. I have made very few changes to the original version published in Spanish in Mexico (Era, 1981). I have introduced the corrections I made in the Catalonian edition published in Barcelona (Empúries, 1985), and others that were made in the English version, thanks to the comments and help of Bertha Ruiz de la Concha. I have added an entirely new section in the form of a *postscriptum* at the end of the book, one that includes reflections on recent events, whereby the contemporary nature of my interpretations may be appreciated by the American reader. Now that I have had the experience of living in the United States for long periods, I could also add that my reflections can, to a great extent, be applied to this country. Although my book is inserted in the critical European and Latin American tradition, it links up with the present cultural and political concerns of the United States, particularly the so-called postmodern condition (which has become a curious bridge between the Old World and the New one). Marginal subculture and minority group issues are now more important than ever in the United States, set as they are within the context of a society which finds it difficult to acknowledge its multicultural nature. The imagery associated with terrorism, the collapse of communism, the limits of democracy, and the limited wars are major issues that are dealt with in this book and around which have become articulated the concerns involving the end of the millennium in the United States.

Anthropologists, historians and sociologists in this country are gradually beginning to appreciate the usefulness of the free essay, a genre which opens the doors to those opaque and difficult areas of knowledge. After the great failures of the "specialists"— sovietologists and orientalists, for instance—who were not only unable to foresee, but failed to prepare for the new course that contemporary history was taking, it is important to recognize in the essay tradition—that begins with Montaigne—a value that academic studies have denied. A great number of friends have helped me to understand that times are changing in the United States, and they have contributed to my better understanding of this country's intellectual and political life. Thanks to their teachings, I was able to write the final pages of the *postscriptum*. I would like to point out the encouragement given me by Manuel Durán, Coco Fusco, John Gillis, Guillermo Gómez-Peña, Luin Goldring, Marco Vinicio González, Gilbert M. Joseph, David Kaimowitz, Florencia Mallon, Gerardo Otero, Alejandro Portes, Roger Rouse, Steve Stern, Dorothy and Edward P. Thompson, Marlie and Mark Wasserman. Conversations with these friends and many others have encouraged my hope that imaginative essays and the rupture of traditional frontiers are opening new spaces to help us understand the world's journey into the next century.

The Imaginary Networks of Political Power

Introduction

At times of transition and crisis we seek beyond the theoretically closed and relatively coherent universes that guide political life. Parallel Lanes may help us out of the ports of traditional political science. We accept the challenge and navigate the turbulent waters of the contemporary State crisis with the help of sails borrowed from the new political imagery. The following essays attempt to establish subtle connections between many unusual themes, commonplaces and well-known political phenomena: namely, structuralism, Eurocommunism, marginal sects, Stalinism, terrorism, detective fiction, apocalypse, neoconservatism, socialist economy, cartomancy, thanatopraxis, ethnopsychiatry, silent majorities, psychoanalysis, Marxist crisis, new philosophers, formal democracy, religion and madness.

An element linking these essays is the reflection on what is by now a cornerstone of modern political interpretation; the problem of *State and power expansion,* which is also an ideology intent on darkening deeply hidden aspects of social life at the close of this century. These essays are strung together within the implied context of dissimilar political moments oscillating between the classic situation of a relatively autonomous guardian State—*apparently* detached from a capitalist society based on free competition—and the extension of State functions to large social sectors dominated by capitalist monopolies—whereby the *appearance* of a fusion between State and civil society is created. These political moments shift between the State's actual omnipresence in socialist societies, where there is *indeed* a fusion between politics and civil life, and the idea of a new socialist situation stemming from the contradictions within socialism as we know it, in which there exists an *actual* severance between the near extinction of the State and an expanding society.

These essays are mainly concerned with the link between the State's new social functions—which produce curious declassing and social mobility phenomena—and the real or imaginary struggle between the so-called marginated and the silent majority. A full understanding of the modern State's legitimacy and reproduction mechanisms must go beyond the concept of social processes as adaptational devices between civil and political society (i.e. "basis" and "superstructure"), and this includes the complex determination relationships "in the last instance" between both. The study of the hegemony of a social class (or fragmented groups conforming a class) over the rest of society calls for the definition of a group of institutions, social relationships and ideas which share the characteristic of being part of a mediating network. Each element in this mediating structure fulfills various functions, of course, whether economic, social, political or ideological. On the whole, however, their particular property is to become a means of transposing class contradictions and conflicts to an imaginary network that gives coherence, unity and stability to society. I should perhaps warn the reader here that certain concepts, particularly those like *silent majority* and *marginality,* are essentially metaphorical; that is, I do not intend to define precise social groups as such, but will refer to their teleological and imaginary derivations and to their consequent political effects. This is not to say that the concrete struggles carried out by various "marginal" groups are regarded as depraved or as deviations within the class conflicts, since they are merely destined to confer legitimacy to a dominating system. On the contrary, these struggles have been known to become precious breeding ground for experiences and new alternatives. I would also like to point out that mediating networks are the stage where class conflicts are *transposed* to a realm where contradictions seem to cancel each other out, but are by no means a real substitute for social struggles. The term *transposition* is used here in its Freudian sense.

The criticism contained in these essays is, in a sense, aimed at conceptions nurturing the development of an immanent world of imaginary networks that entrap modern man and ensure permanent capitalist domination. Let us briefly imagine, however, the possibility of introducing the very weapon of imagination into this criticism. Art does this often enough, so why not extend its strategy into politics, where imagination is so often trapped in its own network and where images are surrounded by walls made up of signs? For this very reason, concepts used here become midway metaphors between science and imagination, material processes and ideological fiction. By translating *method* into an open *style* I trust the discourse will convey the critical situation of the theoretical and practical areas being explored. Here emerges a close, though not obvious, link between Adela Trueta's twenty-two drawings and the twenty-two essays.

This book is, therefore, a cluster of loose ends: each essay and each drawing attempts to make a statement, even as each leaves the path open to the imagination. I suspect the outcome is closer to a basketful of heterogeneous snakes than a rounded off theoretical world. The uncertain task allotted to each reader is to pick out of the basket what is particularly needed or desired; no reader can remain at ease with any one idea picked out of the basket since the possibility remains that it is a kind of snakebite disguised as a joke.

I The Omnipresent State

(The Juggler)

"I am the Alpha and the Omega," says the Lord God, who is, who was, and who is to come, the Almighty.

Rev. 1:8

The dominant image of power and State in the western world emerges as a *revelation* that began as a detailed account of the sufferings undergone by a heterogeneous *marginal* mass of madmen, prostitutes, prisoners, vagabonds and terrorists; of declassed, indigenous and diseased people. The new dominant political philosophy appears under a guise similar to that of the primitive Christian doctrine established by a persecuted and ragged people who bred apocalyptic visions in Asia Minor.

I will start off with the following double confirmation: in the first place, there is no doubt whatsoever that the very fringes of society establish precisely the main outlines of a given society's characteristic repression mechanisms; in second place (and less obviously), the ideology inspired in or supported by the link between the normal and the abnormal, between periphery and center, provides clues that may explain the origin and development of the legitimacy required by a modern system of capitalist domination and exploitation.

I am particularly interested in exploring the latter problem since I am convinced its study will contribute to a further understanding of the complex *transposition* process of social elements which are contradictory and conflictive, profound and irreducibly antagonistic, and of their *substitution* by a dialectic apparatus that *expresses* contradictions on a mediating normal and marginal pole axis.

The new prophets hear—as St. John did on Patmos Island—trumpet calls urging them to discover, behind the tribulations of the marginal rabble, an immense power spread throughout society. It is a power that is nothing but power, that has no center or periphery; no class, racial or cultural borderlines. This absolute power is expressed at every level, whether by oppressors or oppressed, and leaves no virgin land vis-à-vis the State's omnipresence. Unlike the classic political bourgeois philosophy, this curious theory—created from the rags of the marginal world—establishes that both power and State are not placed above society. According to this theory, power *is* society.

As a representative of the most sophisticated French version of this theory, Foucault is a good example of political revelation. In his engaging study concerning the origin of prisons and of modern penitentiary systems he declares that punishment in the modern world becomes a judgment of the "soul," as opposed to medieval punishment conceived as the judgment of the body and manifested through torture. The modern world can only "punish the soul" instead of the body when it *knows*—that is, *creates*—the soul in terms of the power exerted over a punished or guarded marginal body. According to Foucault:

> This need for punishment without torture was first formulated as a cry from the heart or from an outraged nature. In the works of murderers, there is one thing, at least, to be respected when one punishes: his 'humanity.' The day was to come, in the nineteenth century, when this 'man,' discovered in the criminal, would become the target of penal intervention, the object that it claimed to correct and transform, the domain of a whole series of 'criminological' sciences and strange 'penitentiary' practices.[1]

Foucault is right. The bourgeoisie does define itself and create its own world by defining marginal minorities, abnormal beings and deviations; thus, punishment becomes the creation of the soul of the bourgeois consciousness. Foucault has taken these facts and developed what is known as the "political economy of the body" or "political anatomy," whereby deeply-rooted power relationships can be explained in terms of the ceremonial that binds punished bodies to the dominant society. He concludes that "In short, this power is exercised rather than possessed; it is not the 'privilege,' acquired or preserved, of the ruling class, but the overall effect of its strategic positions—an effect that is manifested and sometimes extended by the position of those who are dominated."[2] This is to say that power

---

1. Michel Foucault, *Discipline & Punish: The Birth of the Prison*, New York: Vintage Books, 1979, p. 74.
2. *Ibid.*, p. 26.

relationships "go right down into the depths of society, that they are not localized in the relations between the state and its citizens or on the frontier between classes and that they do not merely reproduce, at the level of individuals, bodies, gestures and behavior, the general form of the law or government."[3]

The problem I am interested in is the logical formulation of a *general* and *global* theory of power, derived from the structural link between the punished marginal body and the domination exerted over it. This power is not the kind exerted by groups of institutions and apparatuses that strive to subject the "citizen" to a given State, nor is it the kind exerted by a group or class over others in a domination system. Foucault's most recent work on sexuality continues along these very lines. It is worth pausing here to point out the main aspects of Foucault's definition of power, since they are fundamental to this new and expanding ideology.

The starting point for the "revelation" of this new theory of power is to think in terms of "sex without the law and power without the king." (*"Penser à la fois le sexe sans la loi, et le pouvoir sans le roi."*[4]) Unlike the traditional bourgeois idea rooted in Hegel, there is no question here of seeking chains of *transcendence* that may link the immediacy of sexual and economic life to the sovereign authority of the State to be found above society. Power is, on the contrary, *immanent* and omnipresent. According to Foucault:

> Omnipresence of power: not because its privilege is to regroup everything under its invincible unity, but because it is being produced at every moment, at every point, or, rather, in every relation between one point and another. *Power is everywhere; it is not that it encompasses everything, but it comes from everywhere.*[5]

Confronted by an opaque reality, the new prophet Foucault *reveals* the essence of power through the martyrology of madness, illness, prison and sex. He is right, although he is also contriving a great imaginary stage where actors and mimes are gathered to represent a comedy. He is right, although he has also prepared a trap. For

3. *Ibid.*, p. 27.
4. Michel Foucault, *Histoire de la sexualité, 1: La volonté de savoir,* Paris: Gallimard, 1976, p. 120.
5. *Ibid.*, p. 122. Emphasis added.

he has built a model of an ideological apparatus in which the most subversive and dissolute impulses of the criminal and the schizophrenic are transformed into a structuralist logogriph of immanent power. This, in fact, makes for a political program summed up in the following septenary:

1) Power is a multiplicity of force relationships immanent to the domination in which they are exerted.

2) Power relationships are not external but immanent to economic processes, knowledge and sexual relationships.

3) Power is not acquired, seized or shared.

4) Power comes from below; no binary opposition can exist between dominators and dominated.

5) It is pointless to seek a general staff that presides over the rationality of power, the governing caste, or groups controlling the State apparatus.

6) Where there is power there is opposition; that is why the latter is not external to power.

7) Opposition is invariably a passive counterpart to the leading domination and is condemned to an endless defeat.[6]

This is, quite obviously, a conservative, demobilizing and pessimistic program. My intentions, however, are not to embark on a lengthy criticism of Foucault's ideas. What I do wish to underscore and undermine, though, is the mechanism inducing him to create a model of the omnipresence and immanence of power, since this will uncover important elements that may explain the emergence of a new ideology. Foucault accepts—as a *fact* to be interpreted—the bourgeois dichotomy that defines marginal and abnormal segments, and then goes on to observe its evolution. The borderlines separating the insane from the sane, the criminal from the innocent citizen, are imaginary; although it is true they become crystallized and materialized in asylums or prisons, according to varying historical conditions—meaning that each culture and society produces its own abnormalities. Such a clear-cut outline of repression, however, plucks out its own roots, so to speak, because the actual social segments locked in antagonistic contradiction—a struggle which is the very motor of repression and thereby poses a "danger" of self-

6. *Ibid.*, pp. 123ff.

destruction—are substituted in this dichotomic normal-abnormal model by chains of signs, ceremonies, messages and symbols. These are perceived and studied in areas of modern life that become barely decipherable dark shadows or shapes. These areas have curious characteristics of their own, best described by means of an analogy with black holes and entropy zones within society.

The black hole of the normal and healthy "silent majority" would be similar to those black points in the cosmos—matter in a state of implosion—discovered by astronomers. The marginal underworld entropy zones, on the other hand, would be in a state of increasing disorder, to be deciphered mathematically in terms of the degradation of energy. This is the process to be followed: a) the normal-abnormal division of society should be proved in accordance to the way the dominant and historically determined ideology defines it; b) the classification is reverted to a real situation, after which the normal and marginal segments (black holes and entropy zones) are placed within sociological and historical contexts; c) the message and formulas derived from these segments are decoded and interpreted; d) a common logic, structural coherence and, by extension, an immanent network of power relationships is revealed.

This model cancels the class contradictions by means of a Freudian substitution and transposition rather than by a Hegelian dialectical mediation. Foucault's model reflects, in fact, what I have termed *the non-Hegelian universe of politics.*[7] Unlike the Hegelian model in which the *dialectic* itself "proves" social contradictions have been overcome, this can now be "proved" *empirically*. Once the segments or spheres of social reality have been structurally dissected, the actual deciphered data reveal the existence of an immanent network of power relationships. At this point, the Hegelian dialectic can be introduced again without the interference of annoying antagonistic contradictions. Foucault actually does introduce it again, although merely as a literary device.

The structural dissection of segments in this model should be carried out as follows: the dominant classifying message should function as a starting point, although it is interpreted according to the signs used to express it; the point of departure is the normal-

7. Roger Bartra, *El poder despótico burgués*, Mexico: Ediciones Era, 1978.

abnormal dichotomy in terms of what this *means* during a certain historical period, and is interpreted according to its *signifiers,* pointed out by McLuhan's dictum "*the medium is the message.*" The question is how to locate those *media* to be deciphered; the way to do it is through the *dominant system's classification and order of these very messages.* This hardly matters when the aim is to decipher the deep— though not explicit—meaning of a signifier. The point here is that there is *another* message, quite different from the one related to the media. And it is precisely at this point that substitution and transposition come in, as this leap—impeccable from the empirical method's viewpoint—from the *dominant* signified to the signified *revealed* by decoding the signifier, has brought about the loss of an essential element: that of *domination.* Signs appear and disappear, as do the masks of a skilled magician, whose actual face is concealed; thus there is no face, only a series of masks. Instead of a signified implying domination there emerges the signified implying the revelation of a "new reality" in which power crumbles into infinite fragments that could be, if so desired, dialectically linked.

A *mediation* has thus been reached—similarly to what occurs in Hegelian logic—which blurs the outline of antagonistic contradictions. A different route has been followed, nevertheless; bridges have been built from one irreducible structure *to* another, whereas the Hegelian dialectic builds bridges *with* these very structures, not conceived as such but as spheres or instances that can be transcended.

My interest here is, above all, to point out that theoretical processes reflect real ones; in other words, they correspond to objective social tendencies that help legitimize the reproduction of the most advanced capitalist exploitation relationships. The main function of this ideology that serves to legitimize the social system is to build bridges between the State and social classes, between ruling and subordinate ones. There comes a point when bridges criss-cross the entire theoretical space: these bridges (or "force correlations") end up by canceling the very points which established the relationship in the first place. Once the *different and opposite* banks united by a bridge are canceled, the worst part is not that the bridges cease to be bridges (as do the media), or cease to carry traffic, as it were, from one side of the river to the other. The worst part is that the bridges not only lose sight of the banks, but altogether cancel the river itself. The bridge is no longer used for crossing over from one bank to another; it merely *conceals* the river. The bridge becomes, above all, the river's ceiling, since the bridges of the new political philosophy conceal the *contradiction* as well as the *difference,* and warrant the deletion of what could be called the fundamental heterogeneity of society. The two banks stand for the contradiction; the river is the vertigo standing for a fundamental fact of reality, namely, the categorical externality separating both banks and the material identity sealing the particular properties of each.

Perhaps we should refer to an abyss rather than a river, since not only an antagonistic contradiction divides the exploited mass from the small ruling social sector. As the contradiction cannot possibly be mediated, a "space" or "void" exists between the two poles. This is the empty space wherein the imaginary seat of ideology lies, housing the "hyperactive nothingness" of the silent masses that support and legitimize the established power. Perhaps this is why Hegel stated that "it has been shown that there exists nothing that is not a mean condition between Being and Nothing."[8]

Even if ideology is seated within an imaginary theoretical space, it rests quite solidly and firmly on social contradictions within a social reality. It is closer to an objective process than a mere "contagion" or "influence" of dominating class ideology since the latter maintains a relatively strict control of mass media and "mental production," to use Marx's term. It also becomes obvious that the class struggle itself engenders a mediating apparatus of transposition and substitution of functions essential to the reproduction of exploitation and political power. This apparatus creates, as if it were a magician of the modern world, two visible and opposite elements that are immediately prominent: at one end the man of the streets, normal and anodyne, silent and integrated, one-dimensional; and at the other end the marginal man, schizophrenic or criminal, sick or perverted, guerilla or terrorist. Both opposites have a role to play within the apocalypse of total and omnipresent power, although their tragic objective stems from a consistent social mediating and legitimizing structure.

8. G.W.F. Hegel, *Science of Logic,* transl. W. H. Johnston and L. G. Struthers, 2 vols., London: Allen & Unwin, 1929, I:I:C:[1]:obs. 4, p. 117.

II Marginals or the Jezebel Syndrome

(The Female Pope)

"I know all about you and how charitable you are; I know your faith and devotion and how much you put up with, and I know how you are still making progress. Nonetheless, I have a complaint to make: you are encouraging the woman Jezebel who claims to be a prophetess, and by her teaching she is luring my servants away to commit the adultery of eating food which has been sacrificed to idols."

Rev. 2:19–20

Modern developed capitalist societies continuously nurture a series of symptomatic contradictions that determine what could be called the *Jezebel syndrome*,[1] characterized by a constant creation, provocation, stimulation and repression of society's marginal areas. These areas contain aggravated, dominated and exploited classes in addition to certain ruling class segments. In brief, it is a manipulation, refunctionalization and recreation of certain aspects of the class conflicts. These manipulative processes become the powerful ideological apparatus exerting control over the deepest (and potentially revolutionary) forms of social conflict. This apparatus bears a similarity to Jezebel who, pregnant with terror, gave birth to a vast horde of strange beings, including criminals, revolutionaries and madmen.

Philosophers are not the only ones to invoke Jezebel—that paradigm of criminal terror, unrestrained sex, and false prophets. Culture and ruling class politics also irritate the population, at the same time they obtain from society—to a greater or lesser extent—a homogeneity amounting to legitimization. In fact, legitimacy and irritation are two aspects of the same process.

The history of the German Red Army Fraction (RAF) provides the clearest examples of the origin, development and generalization of the Jezebel syndrome. The tragic story of the "Baader-Meinhof gang" is the setting for the imaginary theater whereby Germany has established the boundaries of a static and homogeneous society. There is a remarkale lucidity in the way these actors—typical Brechtian characters—understand their role in the drama. Equally

1. According to the Old Testament, Jezebel, queen of Samaria, spread the popular polytheistic pagan cult of Phoenician and Canaanitic origin, opposing Jewish monotheistic conceptions. Elijah's prophecy that Jezebel would suffer a violent death was fulfilled: obeying Jehu's orders, some eunuchs threw Jezebel out of a window of her palace and her corpse was devoured by dogs.

remarkable is their iron-like decision not to step too far from the rules of the game, despite awareness of their role. Ulrike Meinhof, that fascinating revolutionary Jezebel, wrote in 1968:

> We Germans know—ever since Freud, Reich and Mitscherlich—that we have more difficulties than others regarding our internalized aggressions, because they have forced us to repress them and we have never had the right to hate those we should hate, such as our parents, our bosses and all those who dominate us. We have hated the Jews and the communists. We cannot hate the Jews anymore, and apparently it is the same regarding the communists. As to the students, the democratic varnish of society prevents it. The proposal then is that we hate the criminals; they become the scapegoats of our present, thanks to which the uneasiness of the political environment can be unburdened.[2]

The landmark for the spiral development of two processes as regards the extreme left-wing *K-gruppen* struggle was 1968. On one hand, there was a rise in terrorism and repression, whereby the opposition is made out to be criminal. This particular process began the night of April 2, 1968 when a bomb exploded, setting two large Frankfurt stores on fire, and was followed by the arrest of Andreas Baader and Gudrun Ensslin who claimed to have provoked the fire as a "protest against the *indifference of society* regarding the Vietnam genocide." The process ended with the kidnapping of Schleyer and the Lufthansa airplane, the Mogadiscio airplane attack, and the Stammheim prison "suicide" of Baader, Ensslin and Raspe. Simultaneously, a theoretical process was developed and followed by the intellectual elite, known as "the new left," spiritually linked to a greater or lesser extent to the Marxist-Leninist groups' struggle.

I do not wish to pause to consider the first process; let it be said merely that Baader and Meinhof became, in fact, the criminal scapegoats which contributed to fulfill the German State's project to mobilize society, drawing it towards the government. The drama's most obvious outcome was that the mass audience at this imaginary dramatization did, in fact, abandon their "indifference," but not in the sense that the RAF had hoped.

2. *Konkret*, 1968.

I will, however, take a closer look at the theoretical and ideo-logical effects of the drama that culminated in Mogadiscio and Stammheim. Its mass audience also consisted of intellectual black hole decoders and entropy calculators who used the outcome of the "war" between a handful of terrorists and the powerful German State to develop their theories. I will take a French example because the French "new left" can observe events from a distance—from the opposite bank of the Rhine—and also because it is familiar with the "temptation of terrorism" without having "made that mistake," and is thereby in a position to establish a "cold" doctrine and to express its theatrical elements with greater clarity.

Jean Baudrillard[3] perceives the German guerilla theater as a way in which the spectacle of terrorism imposes the terrorism of the spectacle. This is to say that in the theater of cruelty—namely the war between terrorist crime and government repression—there are two distinct poles: the challenge of symbolic subversion and the spectacle of repression. Symbolic violence is an imaginary absolute, on one hand; the order of reality is a simulation model, on the other. Let us take a look at the steps followed in Baudrillard's analysis:

1) Terrorists are free from all logic, particularly that of revolu-tionary action, since their entire performance is so utterly suffused with objective defeats it would seem they were deliberately making mistakes. From this viewpoint, terror-ism renounces all power and strength from the outset, de-spite its use of violent means.

2) Terrorism therefore distorts force correlations: all the strength remains at one pole—the State—against which violence is symbolically aimed.

3) The dominant power, firmly anchored in reality, acts out a simulation strategy spectacle by means of which it obtains an objective victory, disposes of the terrorists, and brings about a social cohesion centering round the government "threatened" by terrorism.

4) The simulation model implies the participation of the state apparatus in a spiral of repression hardly distinguishable from the unpredictable nature of terrorism which employs

3. "Notre théâtre de la cruauté," *Liberation,* November 4–5, 1977.

similar methods—although the latter belong to a semi-secret, murky world.

5) The simulation model is a trap. It keeps a series of events in the dark (suicides that seem to be murders and vice versa, strange disappearances, double agents); it is shrewd enough, however, to leave loose ends that may provide a glimpse of the "hidden truth." "Public opinion" is left to seek or produce the *truth,* the *facts,* what is *real,* which has the effect of creating a kind of solidarity block to counteract the *symbolic* and *imaginary* virulence of the terrorist.

6) The outcome mingles symbolic representation and spectacle, crime and repression, subversion and order, the imaginary and the real. What ensues is a situation of uncontrolled reversibility: every actor, every fact is reversible, which means power loses its political definition.

7) Baudrillard claims to have deciphered the mystery of this "theater." His actual words are worth quoting:

The secret lies in opposing the order of the real to an absolute imaginary, absolutely inefficient on a real plane, although its implosive energy, into which all the violence of real power has been sunk, absorbs all that is real. Such a model is no longer in the order of transgression; repression and transgression belong to the old order of law, that is, the order of a *real* system in expansion. In such a system, all contradictions, including inverse violence, merely accelerate expansion. The virulence here comes from the implosion—and the death of the terrorists (or hostages) belongs to this implosive order: the abolition of value, of sense, of the real, at a given point. This point may be infinitesimal, but it provokes an aspiration, a gigantic convexity, such as occurred in Mogadiscio.[4]

The terrorist model provokes "an excess of reality and buries the system under an excess of reality." The touchstone of Baudrillard's model does not lie in the implosion mechanism so much as in the original opposition between the terrorist as the imaginary absolute and State power as the organizer of reality. The actual opposition, in fact, is that of the symbolic marginal and the real

4. *Ibid.*

masses. According to the old order, violence by the masses provokes an explosion—an expansion—of real power, contrary to the symbolic violence of the terrorist that provokes an implosion. The frightening peculiarity of this model is that it corresponds, step by step, to the new ruling class project of post-democratic hegemony; the single difference is that the new simulation model strengthens rather than ruins the system. This strength is derived from the greater social cohesion around the State that is menaced by an "external threat," but more prominently still from the fact that this model is the political crystallization of the imaginary social substances nurturing a new kind of game.

What Baudrillard has deciphered, in fact, is the way the terrorist's *image* links up with the new dominant ideology. He has not, however, explained just how this image is created. Without further ado he accepts the existing signs of the terrorist and interprets them without coming down to reality itself, without proving how the actual terrorists, rather than the signs, operate. Baudrillard is quite happy to accept the sign and the world of the signified,[5] which means he accepts signs as they are—sealed and classified by the dominant system. The latter proposes exactly that: a political model based on symbolic marginal participation and a government that operates in terms of a simulation game.

As a concept, terrorism (and thus marginality too) implies a set of facts and characters whose true coherence only exists for the ruling class. Terrorist factors and characters are an expression of the social contradictions that prevail mainly among aggravated dominated class sectors and in ruling class segments on the verge or in danger—whether in reality or in imagination—of becoming proletarian. In this way the terrorist, separated from the social womb, becomes an imaginary actor who creates the specific ideological effect of an implosion, a phenomenal suction that empties the great dominated majority of all revolutionary content. This actor's role is to absorb and concentrate the revolutionary and subversive elements of the masses, thereby reducing the latter to a skeleton of power and domination relationships without a revolutionary outlet. All revolu-

---

5. Jean Baudrillard, *For a Critique of the Political Economy of Signs*, Saint Louis, Mo., Telos Press, 1981.

tionary processes are therefore transposed to the terrorist's schizo-phrenic, satanic, evil, perverse and abnormal traits. The Jezebel syndrome is engendered by having the ruling class prophets create the image of terrorism and predict its extinction—an absolute imperative for the system's survival. Very often the terrorist is not merely a subversive fragment of the masses who is isolated by dominant thought (and praxis). The special police services belonging to the political apparatus foster the objective aggravation of the populace and ensure terrorist expression. Political *provocation* as a catalyzer of repression is a well-known mechanism.

The terrorist appears as the image of the real enemy, a transfigured image that incorporates various conditions. On the one hand, the terrorist is regarded as an abnormal, dangerous being, surrounded by mystery, and indestructible save by means of appropriate techniques which call for institutions and specialized personnel—particularly as the traditional political power, as such, cannot confront the terrorist. On the other hand, however, terrorists are "lost" amid the masses; they disguise their terrorist facet and appear as ordinary people. Moreover, the image of the terrorist includes transposed petty bourgeois ambitions such as culture, intelligence and capacity, which turn them into "false prophets." As Baudrillard's model shows, the image of the terrorist gradually grows further and further away from the actual terrorist act; the ruling class fosters the development of an entire, highly complex imagery and demonology continuously at work to create and invent the invisible enemy embodied in the abnormal, the marginal.

Note, for instance, how the German State has invited the population to "seek out" (i.e. invent, imagine) the terrorist. According to a newspaper dispatch published in October 1977, the Bade-Wurtemberg police completed and divulged the following identikit picture of the *average terrorist*.

> This terrorist tends to choose a suburban apartment for a dwelling, where he may remain anonymous. He is between the ages of 20 and 35; he often changes his appearance with the help of wigs, glasses, a moustache and a beard. He is generally reluctant to paint his apartment before moving in and has plenty of garage space at his disposal. He pays several months' rent in advance. His apartment furniture is very modest. As

soon as he moves in he changes the locks on the doors. He often refuses to have his name placed at the entrance door. He avoids contact with neighbors and refuses to let them enter his apartment. He leaves home at irregular hours and does not receive any mail or packages. . . .

Clearly, this inconsequential description could fit almost any unemployed or partially employed youth, or any of those typical inhabitants of industrial suburbs in large modern cities; it could also fit the description of students and intellectuals, militants of various political organizations and, in fact, anyone refusing to limit their habits to a routine, to greet the usual neightbors with the usual automatic gestures, or to hold insipid family and colleague get-togethers, and whose behavior is normal, mediocre and colorless. By means of this identikit picture the police are openly inviting people to report suspects, even as it fabricates and propagates a "popular" image of the potentially dangerous marginal segment.

Popular mass resistance has always found a means of expression that supersedes the limits of generalized forms of struggle. There is a gap between these expressions and the popular struggle of the masses, since the former are triggered by a mechanism whereby certain segments of the bourgeoisie are degraded; in other words, there is a "proletarianization" of certain elements within ruling class spheres. These extreme forms of struggle conform to the objective basis that sustains this ideological configuration—created by the dominant power—of the "ideal Enemy," of the imaginary marginal who helps to establish the broad borderlines of a homogeneous, static and bureaucratic society.

Incidentally, the punk protest substituting the old-fashioned hippie trend has unerringly perceived the supremacy of the medium or sign ("how") over the signified ("what") in the definition of the marginal terrorist. The "Sex Pistols" have synthesized this better than many theorists in one of their songs:

> I am an antichrist
> I am an anarchist
> I don't know what I want
> But I know how to get it.

Anonymous Mediocrity

(The Empress)

"I know all about you: how you are neither cold nor hot. I wish you were one or the other, but since you are neither, but only lukewarm, I will spit you out of my mouth."

Rev. 3:14–16

The standardized expansion of individuals that are spread across modern civil society is nothing more than the ideal projection of a petty bourgeois segment—the exact opposite of the marginal terrorist. Whereas the marginal can be regarded as ink tracing the broad imaginary boundaries of mass society, the latter's agglutinating nucleus is modelled from the substance of the "middle class." When this nucleus is conformed by the petty bourgeoisie, it embodies mediocrity and narrow–mindedness; when it is conformed by the "middle class," however, it becomes the empress of immutability and society's hidden potential, the great mediator of contradictions.

The mediating apparatus is conceived as a sociopolitical area that internalizes antagonistic conflicts, which are then projected and expanded—throughout the state and at the heart of the dominated class—by operating as mechanisms that cancel deep conflicts. Within this apparatus, marginals become an intellectualized and illusory version of the real counter power of the workers. This, then, is a transposition of the concept of revolution from a plausible realm to an imaginary one where it becomes impossible to destroy ruling class power. The mediating apparatus is no mere transposition; it is a realm where the populace engenders a bourgeois ideology and the bourgeoisie engenders a "popular" (though *not* revolutionary) ideology.

The above is ensured by objective socioeconomic mechanisms which propitiate the *embourgeoisement* of popular sectors, whereas bourgeois sectors undergo a kind of "proletarianization." Such mechanisms, which I will not go into here, trigger the reproduction of the petty bourgeoisie and of employees (or "white collars"), bureaucrats and intellectuals. Declassing mechanisms such as these tend to shape both actors participating in the imaginary drama we are witnessing: the normalized mass-man versus the marginal enemy.

Both processes (the *embourgeoisement* of the proletarian and the "proletarianization" of the bourgeoisie) converge in that nebulous and intermediate area called "the middle class." Social groups belonging to this area have a curious perception of the class conflicts and the division of antagonistic social poles, since they experience first-hand the vertigo of the abyss separating one class from another and one historical period from another. Whereas in this social area proletarianization is a danger that can apparently be evaded, rather than an unavoidable fact of everyday life, the *embourgeoisement* of the proletariat is far from ensured or predetermined, and becomes a path bristling with obstacles. In fact, there is nothing further away from the "normal-man" and the "marginal enemy" than this "middle class," this heterogeneous area of conflicts and turbulence, where two opposed worlds converge. The concept of "normal" in this sense becomes a mere set of techniques and comforting ceremonies that may eventually stimulate the *embourgeoisement,* whereas the conception of "marginal" becomes the hypothetical leap that may immerse men in a proletarian world without their actually living a day-to-day proletarian life. In the former case, a bourgeois style prevails although no actual bourgeois life is led, whereas in the latter case, a proletarian style prevails although no actual proletarian life is led. The images of the powerless bourgeois, of the revolution without revolutionaries, have their origins here and combine in a mad spiral to create the powerless bourgeoisie, the revolutionaries without revolution, the revolution that does not destroy power, the non- revolutionary proletariat, the revolution from which the proletariat is absent, the bourgeoisless bourgeois life, the proletariatless proletariat life, and so on.

I would like to dwell here on a significant example of the kind of bridge that helps the "middle class" to cross the abyss separating it from the ruling class. The latter creates a range of illusory institutions destined to administer (with economic as well as political benefits) comforting ceremonies and techniques that instill the bourgeois element in the populace and which are genuine secular versions of the Protestant ethic. The example I have chosen revolves around what is known as "The W. R. Borg Complete Practical Psychology Method." This method—marketed by a transnational company—claims, even in such prestigious newspapers as *Le Monde,* to have discovered the "eternal laws of success." When one writes for information, one receives along with a glossy booklet a letter that reads:

> Sir,
>
> Enclosed with this letter you will find the booklet *The Eternal Laws of Success.* Read it carefully, as I am sure it will help you make a definite step towards a better future.
>
> It explains what the Borg Method is about and how, in a mere span of four or five months, you can acquire:
>
> > —excellent memory,
> > —complete self-mastery,
> > —a just and penetrating spirit,
> > —a strong and agreeable personality
>
> qualities that unfailingly lead to success.

The letter is evidently addressed to clients which are taken to be failures, suffering from bad memory, alienated, superficial, weak and unpleasant—qualities standing in the way of success. It is interesting to note that this propaganda is addressed to a public whose objective situation is such that it will not merely accept an implicitly insulting letter, but is, moreover, ready to comply to the rules of the game established by Borg's method (and its price) in order to escape reality. A little further on, a grateful client is quoted as saying: "I had never given any thought to the fact that all men possess the same intellectual faculties and that each person's success depends mainly on the meticulous arrangement of his mental mechanisms." Thank goodness for that! We are not all innate imbeciles; it takes no more than a technical adjustment to make one the same as everyone else! This very client, in a surge of emotion, adds further on: "I am heading resolutely towards a better future and have left behind the mediocre life which I thought my destiny."

The enclosed booklet signed by the mysterious W. R. Borg tells the reader how to follow the example of great businessmen (equated to great ancient thinkers), how to overcome that loathsome situation of finding oneself surrounded by "people who are not worth more than you but who fare better than you," how to become "happy and envied by all." This range of benefits can be obtained by devoting a mere five minutes every day to this new method ("no time loss, no extraordinary effort required"). The method advertises a cure for shyness and guarantees a penetrating intelligence, a strong will, economic benefits, and peer ideological influence.[1]

If one does not reply, another letter arrives 15 days later. This one is written up in far more practical terms, assuring the reader that the Borg method is time-saving and enables "you to do *better* what you do *wrong* today," and warning that the price of the method is going up in a few weeks, so why not accept this bargain today. The interesting thing about the kind of life model offered to the populace is its prototypical nature—therefore diametrically opposed to the marginal—in which all the traits of the mediocre men are concentrated in a superman image. A mere *technique* is enough to multiply what is trivial, what belongs to everyday life, and lead to "Success and Happiness." The super-hero is the petty bourgeois raised to the nth power.

The third letter proves to be the portrait of the "New Man" proposed by bourgeois society to the middle classes:

> What astounds our friends, from the very first lesson, is to clearly see how THEIR BRAIN FUNCTIONS and to confirm that in general very little, A SIMPLE ADJUSTMENT, is necessary to multiply your own value by ten times. This is what General Quérette, Commander of the Legion of Honor has to say: "I am most interested in having become acquainted with the Borg method, so widely known for some time now. Before one uses a shotgun, a calculator or a camera, one can hardly help reading with great care the enclosed explanatory booklet. Each of us has enough willpower to attain our objectives, enough intelligence to find solutions to the problems of our existence, enough memory to retain the recollections we want to keep. But among ten thousand people is there anyone who knows how to use these marvelous faculties? So far there has been no school to show us how this works. The Borg method fills in this regrettable gap and should be seen as the explanatory booklet, THE INSTRUCTIONS FOR USE OF ALL OUR INTELLECTUAL FACULTIES. . . .

1. All this for 560 francs . . . about a third of the French minimum monthly salary.

The kind of man proposed here is surprisingly symptomatic: a sort of robot with a camera for a head (memory, penetration), a calculator for a heart (a just spirit, efficiency, benefits), and a shotgun for an arm (strength, congeniality), who merely needs to retrieve a mislaid part of his own mechanism by means of this explanatory booklet written by "experts," and embark from there on his irrevocable advance towards success. For the middle class man suspended between the danger of becoming a participant in the impoverished anonymous mass and the anxiety caused by his ambition to climb the social ladder, everyday life is defined here as a detrimental state of solitude, shyness, frustration and mediocrity. But *these very characteristics* can be ordered anew, adjusted and raised to the nth power, so that solitude is transformed into an "affirmation of personality," shyness into "congeniality," frustration into "perseverance" and mediocrity into "optimism."

A process such as this favors conditions that lead to the relatively spontaneous and automatic production of the dominant ideology among the subordinated classes. This can only happen by means of the crystallization of social types in which actual social mobility processes are taken to extremes. The very same way the marginal terrorist embodies the unfettered continuity of proletarianization, the Success-man (normal, steadfast, persevering, agreeable and optimistic) is the resplendent extension of the *embourgeoisement*. Nevertheless, one is the proletarianized bourgeois and the other is the *embourgeoisé* proletarian; after all, these characters stand at the very end of the imaginary extension of real paths. The political and cultural area of the "middle class" becomes a converging point for the improbable possibility of the proletarian class becoming bourgeois and the impossible probability of the bourgeois becoming proletarian. The bourgeoisie cannot, as such, become proletarian, although its younger sister, the petty bourgeoisie, can. And for the ruling class, this danger becomes a borrowed *probability* that nurtures its cohesion. Notwithstanding, the probability of poverty becomes the permanent bourgeois and petty bourgeois nightmare that spawns the myth of the marginal terrorist who threatens to overthrow the capitalist empire.

The embourgeoisement of the masses, on the other hand, is the sweet reassuring dream of the powerful class, although this dream is simply a means of propagating this cushioning effect provided by the middle class. Both the above-mentioned imaginary actors correspond to actual social groups and are, in a sense, marginal, although in relation to society's internal rather than external borderlines; these are the intellectuals and bureaucrats, which is to say workers with a bourgeois head, and bourgeois with proletarian hands. The former are paid to think for the ruling class, the latter are bourgeois working for society. Intellectuals and bureaucrats alike form an elite that consolidates the so-called "middle class," to which employees and the petty bourgeoisie also belong. Both these social groups are related to (and are an extension of) modern society's two main antagonistic social classes: the working class and the bourgeoisie.

The growth and expansion of mass employees and petty bourgeois (and their corresponding bureaucracy and intellectualism) has the effect of solving, continuing and mediating both social poles. One of these effects is precisely to engender the two prototypical actors: the marginal—a hallucinatory absorption of petty bourgeois and intellectual elements—who has embarked on an imaginary journey towards the anti-bourgeois world; and the normal-man who embodies an accumulation of employee and bureaucratic traits, who has also embarked on an imaginary journey towards the anti-proletarian world. The anti-bourgeois world is not proletarian and the anti-proletarian world is not bourgeois; similarly, the marginal is not proletarian and the normal-man is not bourgeois. But both participate in the class struggle drama that becomes an imaginary substitute for real battles.

IV   *Beinflussungsaparat*

(The Emperor)

Each of the four animals had six wings and had eyes all the way round as well as inside.

Rev. 4:8

I would now like to look at the ways the normal-abnormal borderline ideology operates. To this end I will make use of the following hypothesis: sociopolitical declassment and transposition processes bring about effects of immanent and omnipresent power.

These immanent and omnipresent effects usually come hand in hand with a great explosion of signs, signals, symbols, models, simulations and hallucinations, from which our two prototypical actors emerge: the normal-man who represents the silent majority and the marginal who represents the terrorist—or, at any rate, the "loud minority." The decoders of quasars and entropy calculators, however, have discovered in this very explosion the omnipresent power networks in which men are enmeshed. This structure is a deceptive and mytical apparatus persecuting men and causing curious effects; for instance, by inducing hallucinatory images, producing and seizing ideas and feelings through obscure means, motivating actions that tend to undermine their own power, and by engendering strange sensations and illnesses.

What I have just described is the famous *Beinflussungsaparat* or "influencing apparatus" described by schizophrenics as the machine used by pursuing enemies and explained in 1919 by Tausk, a psychiatrist close to Freud.[1] There is an extraordinary resemblance between the mechanisms described by psychiatrists or psychoanalysts and those analyzed by structuralist political scientists; these similarities, of course, are the result of the strong Freudian influence on political thought. Nevertheless, there are also entirely unrelated

1. V. Tausk. "Uber die Entstehung des Beinflussungsaparates in der Schizophrenie," *Zeitschrift für ärtzliche Psychoanalyse,* vols. 1–33, 1919. (Translations: "On the Origin of the Influencing Machine in Schizophrenia," *Psychoanalytic Quarterly,* II, 510, 1933; *De la génèse de l'appareil à influencer au cours de la schizophrénie,* Paris: Petite Bibliothèque de Psychanalyse, 1958.)

resemblances. There are undoubtedly two crucial factors in the explanation of psychic illnesses: the objective situation of the diseased
within the social context, and the prevailing classifying ideology
used when analyzing a patient. It is obvious in many cases that both
patient and doctor use current political images in the description
and interpretation of symptoms; the transposition of what are, in
fact, ideological (social) mechanisms to the clinical realm means that
the scientific explanation of a clinical picture of schizophrenia often
comes close to the analysis of an ideological-political process.

Let us consider our hypothesis and suppose that when the
schizophrenic—the marginal and abnormal par excellence—crosses
the borderline separating him from normality, he makes an interesting discovery. Rather than cutting himself off from reality, the
schizophrenic has been engulfed by it and has lost his identity. Let
us suppose that when he faces what he will later interpret as an
aggression—which very probably was one—the membrane separating the "Ego" from the external world is torn, canceled. This is what
is known as the *loss of the limits of the Ego*. As Tausk states:

> People suffering from disorders complain that the entire world
> is aware of their thoughts, that their thoughts are not enclosed
> within their head but scattered around the world, and thereby
> develop simultaneously in every head. A disordered person has
> lost all consciousness of a psychic entity, of an Ego possessing
> limits.[2]

This state is similar to a specific stage in child development in
which every sensorial stimulus a child comes across is regarded as
endogenous and immanent; this period is prolonged until the child
can tell the first lie successfully, at which point the child realizes
there is a borderline between what he or she *knows* and what other
outside think.

The psychological process is identical to the ideological one
which is not exclusively (or mainly) made up of lies, but also, and
above all, by truths that seem evident because no borderline seems
to separate us from them. An ideology becomes such not only because it is engendered by a social class to represent its interests, but

2. *Ibid.*

also because it *develops simultaneously in every head.* It may seem amusing that ideology should operate in a similar way to schizophrenia, but I am afraid to say that it is, in fact, the interpretation of schizophrenia that has an ideological content. This does not apply solely to the interpretation, since the paths leading to madness are in no way alien to the processes of social oppression and ideological repression. It has been proved that paranoids react to a symbolic construction of the surrounding repressive characteristics of society, rather than to a pseudoreality.[3]

The schizophrenic perceives the "influencing apparatus" as a machine that persecutes him, which bears a similarity to a declassed individual's vision of his oppressive surroundings. In both cases there is no perception of the *external* character of the oppression since the subject has moved away—whether in actual fact or through an imaginary process—from boundaries that previously delimited him or her self. The *embourgeoisé* proletarian and the proletarianized bourgeois perceive a network of immanent power that crushes them when they discover they have been transposed to a social milieu that is *alien* to them but in which they are inevitably immersed. It follows that the middle classes, confronted with the extraordinary growth of the modern State apparatus, should create a social nucleus stimulating images together with myths of total and immanent power. These are the very characteristics of the Deleuze and Guattari model;[4] the transition from an ancient State—a *transcendent* superior unity that integrates relatively isolated and codified subgroups—to a modern State—a product of an immanent law in a realm of decoded flux. "The State is desire transferred from the tyrant's head to the heart of his subject."[5] This is to say that men are dominated not through any manipulation from "above" but because they *desire* it, because they seek a deeply-rooted pleasure. The State would be like the emperor whose gestures of power were fashioned from his subjects' bodies.

---

3. Edwin Lemert, "Paranoia and the Dynamics of Exclusion," in *Human Deviance, Social Problems and Social Control,* Englewood Cliffs, N.J.: Prentice-Hall, 1967. On the other hand, several studies prove the correlation between psychosis-dominated class member, and neurosis-ruling class member.
4. Gilles Deleuze and Felix Guattari, *Capitalisme et Schizophrénie: L'Anti-Oedipe,* Paris: Minuit, 1972.
5. *Ibid.,* p. 262.

If we regard the schizophrenic influencing apparatus as equivalent to the State apparatus, we will find Tausk's classic text to be a modern political philosophy manual. The influencing apparatus would be a projection of the diseased body onto the external world caused by libidinal repression. Could one possibly refer to the State as a morbid projection of a repressed social libido? At any rate, it is a fact that some State *images* are a projection of certain "diseased" social layers in terms of their own position within the social structure. They are "diseased" as they exist within the mediating space of antagonistic contradictions, a space that can merely engender—no matter how effectively—illusions of mediation that originate ideological fiends with "eyes all the way round as well as inside."

It is precisely because "morbid" declassing phenomena do occur in these mediation areas that the ideological effects of immanent and omnipresent power, ideology and repression, continually emerge there too. Althusser has stated that "if eternal does not mean transcendental to the whole of temporal history (which is temporal) but omnipresent, trans-historical, and, therefore, immutable as regards form within history as a whole, I will rephrase Freud's expression: *ideology is eternal,* the same as the unconscious."[6] Psychoanalysis inspired Althusser's interpretation of ideology as an imaginary transposition of the relationship between *individuals* and production relationships. In other words, ideology "develops simultaneously in every head," bearing a similarity to the schizophrenic's conviction described by Tausk.

Possibly the best explanation of the process of ideology production is given by Freud. His analysis of dreams can be translated into the realm of social ideology production, which in a sense means that Freudian analysis should be situated once again within its original context. Freudian interpretation speculates on the mediating socio-ideological mechanisms and their transfer to the realm of the psychic apparatus. Freud not only analyzed his patient's dreams and nightmares but carefully observed modern and ancient civilizations, in addition to the great dreams revealed by religion, literature, art, philosophy and politics.

6. "Idéologie et appareils idéologiques d'État," *Positions,* Paris: Editions Sociales, 1976, p. 101.

The initial resemblance between the nature of dreams and ideology—quite specifically that of the *mediating apparatus*—is the distinction between manifested contents and latent ones. Ideological mediation comes into being if it represents a network of ("true" and/or "false") ideas within a structure that conceals yet another network of ideas and/or facts. In second place, the mediating apparatus is an imaginary, disguised, or frank fulfillment of unsatisfied needs and desires. This implies that the solution to social and everyday life contradictions must be provided by means intrinsic to the actual mediating apparatus, thus creating a solution that remains outside the contradiction-producing realm (thereby remaining a pseudosolution). The desires and needs of consumption, gain and domination may undergo—insofar as they are only partly or fully satisfied—a process of ideological production and manifest themselves as mediators. This process could be defined by somewhat modifying Freud's words: ideology production is never creative, it never imagines anything on its own, it neither judges nor reaches conclusions. It compresses, displaces and classifies the raw material of ideology—striving for sensorial representation—and finally takes on the task of organizing the whole. One may be tempted to regard all those elements appearing as ideology contents as the result of purely intellectual activity. Analysis proves, however, that operations carried out by the spirit are similar to the latent thoughts of ideology which has done no more than reproduce them faithfully.[7]

In other words, the scientific or philosophical justification of class interests has been previously developed; what makes it specifically ideological is not a matter of addenda or change, but of its translation into a language and its transferral to a setting that enables (and induces) the imaginary fulfillment of unsatisfied needs and the explosion of contradictions under controlled conditions.

---

7. Freud's original phrase is as follows: "this elaboration (of dreams) is in no way creative; it does not develop any fantasy of its own, it does not judge nor conclude anything and its function is limited to the condensation of given material, to shift it and to make it apt for the visual representation; all of these activities to which the last bit is inconstantly added, that of interpretation. We also found something in the content of dreams that we would like to consider as a result of a different and more elevated intellectual function, but analysis always convincingly proves *that these intellectual operations have already taken place in the ideas of dreams, since the dream content has limited itself to harboring them.*" Sigmund Freud, *Die Traumdeutung*, Leipzig and Wien: Franz Deuticke, 1900. Emphasis in the original.

Thus the four classic mechanisms characterizing "dream work" can be easily applied to the ideological mediating apparatus: 1) *Condensation,* or the formation of unique images that fuse contradictory ideas and situations. 2) *Displacing,* whereby what is secondary becomes primary and vice versa, and elements can be transposed. 3) *Symbolic disguising,* which is to say the creation of symbols or actors representing actions rejected in reality. 4) *Coherent representation,* which implies that condensed images, transpositions and symbols are ordered and structured into coherent groups. Freud admitted his dream-interpretation chart bore a resemblance to demonology; moreover, the political nature of his analysis becomes obvious, particularly when "censure" is the main cause for dream-induced distortions of reality. Dreams resemble the ideological mediating apparatus in that they are the guardians of sleep, rest and organism reproduction. According to Freud:

> By these means they do nothing more than behave like the most conscientious night watchman, who fulfills his duty by first attempting to stop perturbations, to prevent his neighbors' sleep from being interrupted, but who continues faithful to his duty by waking them up the moment the causes for the disturbance seem suspicious and he is unable to stop them through his own intervention.[8]

The main problem is the fusion of contradictory class interests; in order to create such an illusion, the mediating mechanism is released as a means of "overcoming" repression, of freeing itself imaginarily from the contradiction arising from a need and its satisfaction, as a means of satisfying frustrated desires. A key to the "legitimacy" of a system that harbors antagonistic contradictions is undoubtedly the mediating apparatus which (similarly to dreams) establishes a cultural link between the psychic and the ideological apparatus. The permanent, external and immanent character of ideology cannot be proved except by means of an analogy with the psychic apparatus described by Freud. It is just possible that the legitimizing—and mediating—cultural agent linking ideological and psychic apparatuses may disappear, given the absence not so

8. *Ibid.,* p. 57.

much of "unsatisfied desires" (a permanent element), but of antagonistic social contradictions that require mediation. The analogy between the social and ideological mediating apparatus and the psychic apparatus ceases to operate as soon as we remove its main conditioning elements: namely, a contradiction-plagued organism (in which needs and desires are repressed as well as unsatisfied) which grows and reproduces thanks to these selfsame elements. The basic conditioning element is the actual *connection* between reproduction and repression (between Eros and Thanatos?), in which case reproduction is ensured through contradiction. It is, nonetheless, quite possible to envisage a society in which reproduction and repression are entirely dissociated and about to be extinguished. In fact, any revolution cuts the umbilical cord uniting a system's reproduction mechanism with its repression processes; the revolutionary situation is maintained until a new set of reproduction-repression connections are created.

The privileged spot in Freudian-type dreams—as in the mediating apparatus—lies in those social groups which imaginatively or practically seek (and sometimes manage) to overcome or transcend their class condition and to condense, displace, disguise and order their vital projects which openly oppose a straightforward and disorganized class struggle dilation. The mediating apparatuses are mainly attended and nurtured by a class of men who, seeking transcendence, build an immanent world and fill bottomless seas and rivers with the stones of Freudian demonology. These men dream while they sleep; others, however, daydream, and since their dreams disregard Freudian laws they refuse to fill in with illusions that abyss separating antagonistic contradictions.

V The Minor Philosophers and Their New Revelation

(The Pope)

I saw that in the right hand of the One sitting on the throne there was a scroll that had writing on back and front and was sealed with seven seals.

Rev. 5:1

The French intellectual fashion illustrates how the "middle classes" stimulate the rise of mediation mechanisms and imagery concerning the immanence of power. I am thinking particularly of the "new philosophers" who appear in the eyes of society as enlightened dissident marginals and who have taken up and debased Foucault's fundamental theses, merging them with ancient concepts of the Christian apocalyptical tradition and North American anti-communist political theory dating back to the cold war.

FULL POWER TO THE IMAGINATION!

It is common knowledge that the imagery that best supports a system of exploitation is reaped by the ruling class in areas fertilized by great popular movements. Over two decades after May 1968 and at a time of utmost need, the French ruling class has extracted from the very core of the popular revolt a mystical thought that lends legitimacy to its political hegemony: this is the so-called "new philosophy." Those who back in May 1968 imagined that power should be taken over by their imagination have come to see their wish embodied in the very heart of State domination. It comes as a shock to witness the bitter accumulation of defeats in French leftist history translated with inexorable logic into a handful of minor philosophers[1] who are, all of a sudden, the new watchdogs of the capitalist State!

At the very core of the heterogeneous 1968 movement was a petty bourgeois element. It spread the wings of its imagination, hurling itself in a miraculous flight across the skies of left-wing Maoism, traversing the airs of Palestinian revolution and guerrilla romanticism, descending into the hell of prisons and psychiatric

---

1. Jean-Marie Benoist, Jean-Paul Dollé, André Glucksmann, Christian Jambet, Guy Lardreau, Bernard-Henri Lévy and Philippe Nemo; we could also add their mentor and Christian confessor, Maurice Clavel.

wards, outlining the feminist struggle and the struggle of emigrated workers. By flying over the extreme borderlines of exploitation, at times even bespattered by the mire of class struggle, its political discourse actually translated real violence into an imaginary war between the marginal underworld and the normalized entirety of bourgeois society. Reality was inverted through this discourse so that the ruling minority became the organic, one-dimensional mass of *embourgeoisé* society, whereas the exploited mass became a minority group of political clusters and marginal movements.

This imaginary flight was threatened by two tendencies: one was the isolation sensed by any authentic revolutionary vanguard—whether rooted in marxism or anarchism—living in adverse conditions; and the other was the isolation felt by a fraction of the petty bourgeoisie that was displaced from its natural context to the heart of a popular movement. The latter tendency developed, eventually shaping the "new philosophy" once the minor philosophers returned to their natural home. These minor philosophers, however, did not by any means return with their hands empty; they brought with them, in addition to the disillusion of defeat, a prestige seized from those fighting against the modern Leviathan—the State.

THE SEVEN SEALS

These seven minor philosophers are like the seven seals at the close of the book containing the apocalyptic reproduction of Power, Barbarity, the Prince and the State. The most revealing fact is that their unity as "new philosophers" does not arise from their writings but *is assigned to them by the State, by the ruling ideological apparatus and through mass media.* This "new philosophy" owes its recognition, rather than to the coherence of these philosopher's thoughts or by virtue of their having something "new" to say, to the great princes and mandarins who reign over politics, universities, television, the publishing industry and the press, and who have launched them into the market of ideas. The "new philosophy," however, should by no means be regarded as a passing publicity phenomenon, precisely because its value is assigned by the hegemonic and dominant power, and because it expresses actual political tendencies. These "new philosophers" proclaim with virulence the arrival in the Western and

Latin political-cultural world of an ideological trend that has already come a long way in Anglo–Saxon and Germanic cultures: namely, those theories of *total power* that nourished typical postwar United States and German anticommunism.

It is not coincidental that the "new philosophers" should make their appearance precisely at a time when new Southern European political tendencies have reached maturity. The latter make socialism fashionable and bring about a crisis concerning the status quo which is based on blocks and areas of influence of the Great Powers. The proposals championed by the entire "new philosophy" arsenal are linked to the present political articulation; the four black beasts upheld by the new minor philosophers are the State crisis, the Gulag, the renovation of Marxism, and mass participation in the government.

It is not an interesting task for any "new philosophy" criticism to establish a careful distinction between the Lacanian mysticism of Guy Lardreau, Christian Jambet and Philippe Nemo and Jean-Marie Benoist's conservative eclecticism; or to separate Bernard-Henry Lévy's pessimism from André Glucksmann's pseudo–plebeian faith and Jean-Paul Dollé's Heideggerian indigestion. There is a simple reason for not embarking here on a dissection of the "new philosophy"; namely, that when each philosopher is viewed separately, they have very little to contribute. As Deleuze has said, "their thought is worthless." A criticism of the "new philosophy" can only be a criticism of the State that has engendered it and an analysis of the ideological–cultural articulation it expresses. These philosophers are, in fact, a symptom rather than an illness. Accordingly, we should deal with them as they appeared originally and in terms of how the political-ideological power presents them—despite their complaints that lack conviction and energy—which is to say as a cohesive collision group challenging Marxism and socialism.

The French edition of *Playboy* (June, 1977) published an interview with Bernard-Henry Lévy, the "founder" and "manager" of this group. He claims, next to photos of nude women, that

> successful revolutions always end in a bloodbath. The only
> thing we can do is learn the lesson and organize resistance

against barbaric forces by inventing new committees of intellectuals, anti-fascists and anti-communists. This is the main problem nowadays, far more so than injustice or social inequality.

The *Paris-Match* issue of that same month heralded Glucksmann as the relay of old Christian Maurice Clavel. In September, the cover on *Time* magazine showed a picture of Marx crossed with red and yellow letters that read: *"Marx is Dead: France's New Philosophers Speak Out."* The excitement began when the "new philosophers" introduced themselves as such in the June 1976 issue of *Les Nouvelles Littéraires.* A year later the show began when a well-known television program had Lévy, Glucksmann and Clavel confronted by two critics who had recently published a book entitled *Against the New Philosophy.* A few days earlier, *Le Monde* had published a *dossier* on the "new philosophy" that contained articles in favor and against it. The entire press announced the "great" debate on TV. Both critics, François Aubral and Xavier Delcourt, though not exactly brilliant, launched a harsh attack. The "show" lasted throughout the spring and all self-respecting intellectuals had something to say about it.

THE GULAG AS A PETTY BOURGEOIS NIGHTMARE

A theme that is common to all the "new philosophers" and has endowed their discourse with the *ultima ratio* is their self-appointment as the western version of "dissidence" in socialist countries. The main "evidence" that Marxism is the antecedent and logical basis of totalitarianism lies in Stalinism, the red terror, concentration camps, and psychiatric wards; in other words, the Gulag depicted by Solzhenitsyn. A typical example is provided by the above-quoted Lévy interview in *Playboy:*

> *Playboy:* Are you anticommunist?
> *Lévy:* A primary anticommunist.
> *Playboy:* What scares you about communism?
> *Lévy:* The dream fed on a homogeneous society, without divisions and contradictions. Its plan whereby Power is used to crush society, to reabsorb the division between individuals preserved by liberalism. Totalitarianism in the strictest sense.

Because, you know, the classless society does exist, it is not merely a sweet and unattainable utopia; it exists in the Soviet Union and has the inevitable Gulag for a reply, for its limits or borderlines. If a homogeneous and unified society should be proclaimed, the dissidents of this unity must be placed somewhere, which is why they are behind bars.

This is the great lie that nurtures the "new philosophy," and that springs from a gross deformation of reality; in socialist and capitalist countries repression *invariably* derives from inequality, social division and heterogeneity, and class cleavages. By denying such evidence these minor philosophers establish their right-wing and conservative position as regards the western politics, although they also represent *a reactionary position within the complex struggle carried out within socialist countries.* Only total ignorance (and concealment) of the reality and of the enormous complexity of the struggle going on in socialist countries could convince anyone that life over there is reduced to an almighty State surrounded by a homogeneous social mass of sheep-like men and a small group of select and heroic dissident intellectuals. Every socialist country has *embourgeoisé* layers of bureaucracy, and these safeguard their privileges by inspiring all kinds of petty bourgeois ideas about freedom, human rights, and so on. These very layers contribute (whether voluntarily or not) to the development of dissident sects in the interstices of the State apparatus that confront both the dominant political structure and the popular struggle, providing a model for the lack of individuality among the masses controlled by an overwhelming absolute power. These layers of bureaucracy promote certain kinds of "liberal" measures intended to protect their own privileges and wealth, and to nurture dreams about the western "paradise," which are the examples the "new philosophers" provide.

True dissidence in socialist countries—which is of course fighting to democratize political and economic structures—has deep roots and expresses the interests of privilege–dispossessed and low salary sectors of the mass of workers, as evidenced by Prague's Dubcek period and Poland's opposition worker movement. The difference between both forms of dissidence is that whereas the first expresses the bitterness of lost confidence in the people, the second is rooted in the extraordinary heterogeneity and diversity of the popular mass. The former is a dissident excrescence of bureaucracy; the latter is the rebellion that proclaims the real need for a process whereby the State (and bureaucracy) should come to an end.

The "new philosophers," together with Solzhenitsyn, are expressing those conservative and reactionary dissident sects which exalt the spiritual values of the "Russian soul" (the *mujik* raised to the nth the power) who confronts the proletarian and supposedly bureaucratic mass of the dominant "classless" society. It is no coincidence that many exiled dissidents regard with some perplexity and even distaste this "new philosophy," this western "dissidence" protected and pampered by the State. For them a dissident is, by definition, one who opposes the State and experiences its enmity.

THE STATE: LOVE AND HATRED

The vicious and accumulated misunderstanding encouraged by the minor philosophers reaches an outrageous extreme when they attempt to "prove" that the theoretical justification of the totalitarian State is to be found in Marx himself. Glucksmann sets out to prove this in his book *Les maîtres penseurs.* Jacques Rancière has shrewdly discovered the very roots of the deception:

> Glucksmann becomes more radical when he needs to prove, against all evidence, that Marx values the State in terms of its opposition to private society. The impossibility of finding the smallest of proofs provides the supreme proof: "although the chapter on the State," writes Glucksmann, "had been foreseen, it happens to be missing from *Das Kapital.*" This is familiar Stalinist logic: the best evidence of someone's guilt is the lack of evidence, because when no evidence is available, this means it has been concealed, and if it has been concealed, it means this party is guilty.[2]

It may come as a surprise to find these minor philosophers who condemn socialism for being totalitarian using a Stalinist type of discourse. This curious phenomenon can, nevertheless, be explained by the fact they propose as the real model of modern society those terrifying and phantasmagoric images of socialism fabricated by

2. In *Le Nouvel Observateur*, July 25–31, 1977.

petty bourgeoisie nightmares. The latter is, in fact, both transposition and reversal of the actual petty bourgeois world which is ruled by homogeneity, identity and immanence—"common sense," in other words, that ideal breeding ground for Stalinist discourse. Any deviation from this world becomes automatically *suspect*. Petty bourgeois nightmares invert a self-fabricated design of the universe. Thus they regard socialism as what is, in fact, the petty bourgeois micro—world—magnified to become all-inclusive—in which loathsome aspects are raised to the nth power in terms of what the petty bourgeois lacks in the way of refinement: wealth, bourgeois characteristics, and so on. The socialism depicted by the petty bourgeois is the split image of what he in fact *is* but *does not want* to be—which is to say mediocre, rigid, dense, despicable, mean, stingy, lifeless, boring, repressive. The Glucksmannian minor philosophy, however, preserves the essential prejudice that anything unmentioned and that cannot be "proved" by common sense is suspect. It then follows that if Marx did not develop a state theory this was because he *knew* (but could not admit) that in a socialist regime the State must exert absolute and total domination over society. What is curious about the "new philosophers" is that their hatred towards their own petty bourgeois condition has been turned into a repudiation of socialism. In this sense they are representatives of a "left-wing" Poujadeism. Their mingled love and hatred towards the State is a symptom of the typical petty bourgeois who detests being subjected by the State but manifests this by venting his hatred on a neighboring State (whether German, American, or Soviet) even as he allows himself to be wooed by the state powers of his own country.

MARXISM AND THE RABBLE

A critic from the daily newspaper *Liberation* was partly right when he stated—in a traditional leftist style—that Glucksmann had awakened the realization that the Gulag also exists within our brains. He forgot, however, to add something essential: in our *petty bourgeois* brains. He overlooked the fact that possibly the best refutation of those nightmares created by the minor philosophers had been made twenty years before by Roland Barthes in his article "A few words by Mr. Poujade."

> We know now what the real petty bourgeois is; it is not even
> what can be seen, it is what can be counted; this real, the
> narrowest any society could have ever defined, nevertheless has
> its philosophy: that of "good sense," the famous good sense of
> the "small people," says Mr. Poujade.[3]

As if to confirm this, Glucksmann now declares the value of
the "Copernican revolution developed in the heads and hearts of the
simple people, when they discover their country to be a concentration camp."[4]

Nothing could be further from my intention than to deny (or,
even further, justify) the reality of Stalinist repression processes and
effects. I only wish to point out here that the vision upheld by the
"new philosophy" regarding these phenomena is a diseased reflection
of the terrified petty bourgeoisie, trapped between powerful monopolies and the rise of the worker movement in Southern Europe.

Marxism has been profoundly rejected by the minor philosophers mainly because it "leaves no room" for society's "depolarized
central zones," for the middle class or "rabble," as it has been re-
christened. This *rabble,* unforeseen by Marxism, would be the admixture of marginals exalted by the minor philosophers when the
latter were maoists, and the "middle belt of men who without being
exclusively exploited are not exploiters."[5] This new social substance,
this rabble, is "dissident" rather than revolutionary. It is worth
mentioning that this "middle belt" is very real in France, although
it is in no sense plebeian. Part of it votes left during the first round
of the elections but votes right during the second one. Marxism
aggravates the minor philosophers in the sense that it represents the
worker's power vocation and in the sense too that if, according to
their conception, power is perverse, it becomes all the more so when
originated amid the proletariat since it then contains the embryo of
"communist barbarism." The "rabble," however, at home in their
comfortable and domesticated dissidence, becomes an opaque and
mediocre statism, and thereby contributes to a new development of
the political potential of the ruling bourgeois class. One should,

---

3. Roland Barthes, "A few words about Mr. Poujade,"
4. André Glucksmann, *La cuisinière et le mangeur d'hommes,* Paris: Seuil, 1975, p. 204.
5. André Glucksmann, *Les maîtres penseurs,* Paris: Grasset, 1977, p. 310.

nevertheless, keep in mind that this same "plebeian middle class" presses towards fascist power forms when aggravated by social tensions. Thus, by denouncing a new political apocalypse, the minor philosophers have dangerously invoked forces that have already given full rein to the most dramatic and unbridled repressions in Europe!

VI   Postponed Destiny

(The Lover)

"*Holy, faithful Master, how much longer will you wait before you pass sentence and take vengeance for our death on the inhabitants of the earth?*"

Rev. 6:10

Political legitimacy in a system of exploitation does not arise from an imposition of the wiles and deceptions of the ruling class. Quite obviously, this imposition is true of many cases, although it is not a basic mechanism. The point is not whether power issues from every direction rather than from a "center"— which in any case is merely a matter of appearances. There can, in fact, be no eternal ideological mediation. It could be said that its origin and development resemble a process whereby "immunity" to a certain disease is created through the reproduction of antibodies, or psychic "stability" is achieved through "censoring" and "rejection" mechanisms (as described by Freud). Mediation can be created in the very same way a vaccine (a "false enemy") produces antibodies, or a "censoring" mechanism brings forth in dreams (already filtered, selected and disguised) what is habitually rejected. Thus, in order to make one way of life "immune" to another which may revolutionize it, "limited wars" and imaginary battles are fought against expressly fabricated "enemies" who are distorted projections of real enemies.

The outcome of such battles is that actual forces are weakened, postponed, and temporarily impaired, unfit to undertake major struggles in which antagonistic interests are at stake. Moreover, such battles strengthen the position of the ruling classes, particularly their system of alliances with certain sectors of the subordinated classes.

The transmutation of antagonistic enemies into "weak" and "false" ones—endowed, nonetheless, with a fearsome mask—is not a simple operation of political or literary fiction. "False enemies" multiply along the roads that purportedly lead to freedom, roads that seem to stretch as far as "marginal" extremes and which find their way through the interstices of the opposite ground. This is why I have already related these roads to the mediating processes of the *embourgeoisement* of the dominated and the proletarianization of the dominating, and why I provided such extreme examples as that of the marginal terrorist and the silent majority normal-man. This is a widespread process, however, by means of which contradictions in civil society tend to engender "pressure groups," "subcultures," "ways of life" and "liberation practices"; all the latter steadily secrete innumerable characters called upon to substitute old class struggle actors.

Marginal religious and semi-religious phenomena are particularly pregnant with modern myths engendered from these very roads that purportedly lead to freedom. The new religions are by no means independent from a set of liberation practices which, despite their heterogeneous nature in terms of content and origins, unanimously offer alternatives for coping with the crisis of traditional liberal society. A great many roads leading to salvation take advantage of the apocalyptic images of the war waged between Communist Terror and Liberal Mediocrity (concealed, for instance, in Richard Nixon's Watergate). These roads range from the old philosophic syncretic methods rooted in the East and established by Krishnamurti, Radhakrishnan and Gurdjieff, to the esoteric practices rooted in the West, such as occultism and spiritism, in addition to Rosicrucian, Masonic and Cabalistic societies; they also include astrology, new alchemy and apocryphal religious traditions (Manichaeism, satanic sects and demonology). To these we should add ancient and new oriental—though westernized—techniques such as zen, yoga, fire yoga (agni–yoga), adoration yoga (Bhakti-yoga), knowledge yoga (jnâna–yoga), Chinese meditating gymnastics (T'ai Chi-ch'uan), the aikido, and so on. There are, moreover, many new techniques involving bodily liberation, relaxation and meditation that have generally been developed in the United States. Some of these are: biofeedback (biological feedback that stimulates awareness of and exerts control over heartbeats, brain waves and muscular tension); bioenergetics (a method, created by Reich when the *Beinflussungsaparat* already had a hold on him, whereby anxiety is liberated through painful physical exercise); the Vittoz method (body and sensorial reception brain control); scream therapy (the verbalization of emotional conflicts and blocks); self-hypnosis (relaxation method); *gestalt* therapy (or form therapy, in which the different rejected parts of the body are progressively integrated through a "live" dialogue with a person's contradictions or with the object troubling a person); sophrology (which studies the changes in human consciousness and its organic projections); the more or less ritualistic or mystical use of substances such as LSD, mescaline, psilocybin, cocaine, marihuana, and so on.

A 1973 survey in the United States revealed the existence of over eighty spiritual and therapeutic organizations that propose to lead their followers to "superior states of consciousness."[1]

The new religious sects fuse, in what are probably the most spectacular ways and through rigorously hierarchical organizations, the marginal-man and normal-man myths. Some sects adopt a strange syncretic mixture of new values favored by "marginal" youths, the so-called communitarian hippie subculture, for instance, and highly conservative and reactionary forms of traditional bourgeois ideology, such as anticommunism, puritanism and religious fanaticism. The most widespread of these western sects would be those led by the Korean Sun Myung Moon, as well as the Krishna Consciousness, the Children of God, Transcendental Meditation, the Scientology Church, the Divine Light Mission (headed by guru Maharaj Ji), and the Soka Gakkai. Of the same ilk, though a little older, are the Jehovah's Witnesses, the Mormons, the Baha'ie World Faith, the Adventists and Christian Science. What distinguishes the latter sects from more recent ones is that the "marginal" element is hardly developed, although traditional petty bourgeois traits are enhanced. Millenary sects such as the Jehovah's Witnesses, the Adventists and the Mormons have developed ethical forms along Protestant lines, as well as models of the execrable normal-man, both of which are fully integrated with the mechanisms of liberal capitalism. Nevertheless, certain elements belonging to these sects which emerged in the 19th century have been taken over by the new ones, namely, *millenary and messianic revelation, scientism,* as well as certain *forms of communitarian life* often inspired in primitive Christian life. The new sects usually contribute additional traits, such as a

---

1. Alain Woodrow, *Les nouvelles sectes*, Paris: Seuil, 1977, and Jean-Marie Schiff, *Le livre des pouvoirs de l'esprit*, Paris: Retz, 1976. Most of the descriptions introduced here have been taken from Woodrow's interesting book.

protest against consumer society, an *approach to oriental philosophy and mysticism,* the use of new *psychotherapeutic techniques,* and the development of a *profoundly antiliberal political consciousness.* They engender a new, young, religious, aggressive, fanatic, subversive, dangerous, organized and autocratic marginality which embodies to perfection the "invisible enemy" that evades democratic control. This new millenarianism often manifests itself differently from the traditional one. The latter announces, with greater or lesser precision—although invariably close at hand—the end of the world and the advent of a new earthly kingdom. These sects envisage themselves as resembling that of the ancient Jews; in other words, as D. H. Lawrence put it, "a people of postponed destiny."[2] Yet other new sects believe the new messiah has already arrived or that they form part of the process whereby a new society is being created. Each sect, however, actually fulfills the tragic task of *postponing destiny* and each proposes a way of life and a set of beliefs predating "original sin" (or the moment of doctrinary deviation) that brought about evil. They want to experience, so to speak, the love shared by Adam and Eve *before* they were tempted by the serpent, while they wait for the endlessly postponed arrival of the millennium.[3]

Charles Russell, founder of the Jehovah's Witnesses, predicted the arrival of the millennium for 1914 (which, ironically enough, marked the beginning of war); Joseph Rutherford, his successor, moved the date forward to 1925; and Nathan Knorr, the following head of the Witnesses, set it for 1975. It became necessary, when 1976 began, to explain why the kingdom of Christ had failed to arrive and to declare more cautiously that the end would be here "very soon." The Adventists, who calculated the return of Christ for 1843 and 1844, still await the final destruction of Satan and unrepentant sinners. The more practically–minded Mormons began to build their Holy Zion—where, according to Joseph Smith's revelations, the ten scattered tribes were to gather—in Salt Lake City, with such enthusiasm and efficiency that they practically control all Utah.

2. D. H. Lawrence, *Apocalypse,* ed. by Mara Kalnins, New York: Viking Press, 1982, p. 27.
3. The situation of many left-wing political groups has become similar to that of religious sects.

In contrast, according to the Holy Spirit Association for the Unification of World Christianity, the New Messiah or Lord of the Second Coming is here to complete Christ's mission, embodied in none else but Sun Myung Moon himself. At the end of the Second World War, a young Korean electrician called Moon, born in 1920, member of the Pyongyang Pentecostal Church, gained notoriety as a preacher of a particular brand of Korean Messianism. He was apparently arrested by the communists and, according to him, tortured, before the United Nations Forces freed him in 1950. According to the doctrine of the new church he founded in 1954, it was God's will that Adam and Eve's Union should engender the "perfect family" destined to govern "God's earthly kingdom." It so happened, however, that Lucifer seduced and copulated with Eve, who in turn corrupted Adam; so God's will was that his son Jesus should find a perfect woman and thereby engender a New Humanity, plans unfortunately thwarted by the crucifixion. According to the Bible, the New Messiah destined to sire that new family which would govern the "visible earthly kingdom," was to come from the East, from Korea—and moon is that very man.

The perfect family must establish God's new earthly kingdom by means of a victory over communism, Satan's chief instrument. *The New York Times,* in its September 16, 1974 issue, declared that, according to Koreans who knew Moon in his youth, his arrest by the communists was caused by his "disruption of social order," and, mainly, to "licentious sexual practices." He was arrested again in South Korea, accused of adultery and bigamy, and a third time in 1955 for preaching "sexual rites" in his church. The fact is that Moon began his quest for the "new family" when he left his second wife, settled in South Korea, and married a woman called Choé; she bore him a child who is now in charge of the Unification church propaganda at a Seoul university. When Moon was arrested, his third wife left him; he then lived for a while with another woman, who bore him another child. In 1960, however, he discovered and married the "New Eve": an eighteen-year-old student called Han-hak-ja.

This is, obviously enough, the kind of story likely to cause a scandal among good traditional consciences and make their hair stand on end. An admixture of sex, anticommunism, war and religion has, nonetheless, stimulated the imagination of sect followers and reinforced the complex mythology woven around Moon's life. The sect defined his last wedding as "the wedding of the Lamb," his wife is known as "Mother of the Universe" and their seven offspring the "sinless children." Followers of this doctrine are "members of the family" by extension, and now amount to over two million, spread throughout a hundred or so countries (650,000 in Korea, 50,000 in Japan, 50,000 in the United States). In a matter of years, this sect acquired the same number of followers as the Jehovah's Witnesses or the Adventists, although they are outnumbered by the three and a half million Mormons.

The above-mentioned principles added to the explicit purpose of combating communism and of once again unifying the new Promised Land (Korea)—form the pillars of Moon's church. Each new member is assigned a spiritual father or mother; then there is a head for each family, for each country, for each area, and so on, forming an ascending pyramid with Moon at the apex. This networking makes for an organized multiclassist "subculture" woven around daily frustrations and based on "new" religious, family and philosophical ideas. It is also structured in terms of a profoundly antiliberal (as well as anticommunist) political consciousness. It therefore has the readiness of a medieval castle from which crusaders periodically set forth to exert pressure on the political apparatus of different countries to fulfill the sect's objectives.

Another sect, far smaller, with western roots, and similar to Moon's, is the so-called Children of God or *Jesus Revolution;* their use of "revolutionary" political terminology turns the class conflicts into a war waged by God and Satan. As they see it, Satan destroyed the original harmony in the God-created earthly paradise. Poor and rich embody respectively the principles of Good and Evil; the poor, forever persecuted by the rich, have rebelled ineffectually and have been crushed. In the near future, however, the self-extermination of the rich in an atomic war will liberate the poor who will then rebuild a perfect primitive society. According to them, "the great atomic war soon about to explode will eradicate most rich and industrialized countries in the world, and small agricultural workers will be the sole survivors." Similarly to other sects, the Children of God have organized a project that contemplates an alternative society in which the seed of a future society is supposedly contained; and although they claim to be part of the social struggle they in fact give the impression they are a marginal, persecuted people.

This sect was founded by David Berg in 1969, a methodist ex-pastor who now calls himself Moses, Moses-David or King David. He represents the maximum authority—the same as Moon vis-a-vis his New Age Pioneers—at the apex of a rigid pyramid–like structure in which authority is scaled as follows: David Berg is obviously at the very top; next come his wife Jane, known as Mother Eve, and their four sons and their spouses, known as "bishops." Next in hierarchical descent are the "ancient," the "colony pastors," the "tribe pastors," the "disciples" and, at the very bottom, the "sheep" or newcomers. The Children of God apparently total only six thousand throughout the world, but they have already caused quite a stir in some countries that has brought them to public notice.

Another brand of messianic marginality is to be found in the famous eastern gurus. The most well-known—due to his spectacular personality and his influence (over seven million followers, 80,000 of which live in the United States)—is the guru Maharaj Ji. Born in India in 1958, he is young and extremely fat and rides in a white Rolls-Royce. According to his followers, he has been preaching since he was two and, at thirteen, he began a "Journey for World Peace" to spread his teachings. Guru Maharaj Ji is regarded as

> the perfect Master who has come to this troubled world to deliver us from affliction by revealing the same spiritual meditation that Jesus, Krishna and Buddha revealed, each in his own historical period. The perfect Master reveals four things—Word, Light, Celestial Music and Nectar—and shows us the way to experience them continually through meditation, which is the direct experience of God.[4]

The new sects are singularly inserted in the great scientific and technical revolution of our times. Religious esoterism is mingled

4. Quoted by Woodrow, *Les nouvelles sectes,* p. 184.

with a complex scientifically-oriented symbolism that fulfills and illustrates pressure tactics and technologies of persuasion. Despite the esoteric and messianic bale these sects have in tow, their expansion, organization and propaganda techniques can hardly be called "primitive"; this slickness also applies to the link they usually establish with scientific development. They are a typical product of modern capitalist civilization.

The Christian Science sect, founded by Mary Baker Eddy at the end of the nineteenth century, is a good example of how optimism and blind faith in scientific progress can be absorbed and applied in sustaining a new religious system. Christian Science considers man as a spiritual, rather than a material, entity that forms part of all that exists, namely the perfect God. But man's perfect harmony is destroyed by evil thoughts operating through a "harmful animal magnetism," an idea adopted from Mesmer's studies on animal magnetism. The fact is that this church publishes what is even now one of the most important popular North American journals, the *Christian Science Monitor*.

Moon's Unification Church is a curious admixture of taoist-rooted dualism, yin-yang philosophy, Christianity, and scientism. Moon's "scientific" theories may appear to be—and are, in fact—incredible distortions of modern scientific thought. Although they can hardly be regarded as discourses attempting merely to dupe stupid and ignorant people, they are a frightening fusion of irrational elements in certain modern scientific trends, the faltering discoveries in barely known realms of reality, the spectacular nature of some recent scientific discoveries, and the anxiety and problems of everyday life. All this creates a scientific-religious composite in which complex questions are given simple answers. The Unification Church has organized, by means of certain cultural associations which it sponsors and controls (the International Cultural Foundation, for instance), important scientific meetings. Moon financed one of these in London, in 1974; most of the one hundred and forty guests invited were renowned professors and scientists and included twenty-two Nobel Prize winners. One of them, Lord Adrian (Nobel Prize in Medicine, from Cambridge) stated: "We wish to thank the Reverend Sun Myung Moon for the opportunity he has given us to participate in this conference. He has transmitted, a qualified sage that he is, fundamental ideas that give this meeting direction and which we recognize as valid."[5]

His Divine Grace A.C. Bhaktivedanta Swami Prabhupada, head of the Krishna Consciousness, has also become involved in the scientific realm. He has written a booklet entitled *Antimatter and Eternity,* in an effort to prove the relationship between the discovery of the antiproton—that proves there are two forms of matter (particles and antiparticles)—and that of the soul. His analysis upholds the existence of a world and an anti-world (consisting of antimatter), and that the human soul would be antimatter as opposed to matter. The booklet goes so far as to explain that a Krishna Consciousness devotee can travel to any planet, by means of astanga-yoga. Another of this sect's booklets quotes a discussion that took place in Moscow (!) in 1970 between Prabhupada (a visionary stereotype) and a Soviet orientalist (a "sage" stereotype) regarding the scientific character and infallibility of ancient Vedic teachings. Among their topics is a scientific discussion regarding shit (stereotype of daily life taboos), which I quote by way of an oddity:

> *Prabhupada:* I will give you an example. The Vedas recommend that a bath be taken immediately after touching one's own excrement or an animal's, so that one may purify oneself.
> *Katowski:* That is quite natural; it is simply a matter of hygiene.
> *Prabhupada:* Yes. But, on the other hand, it has been said that cow dung is pure, although it is also animal excrement. . . . Now, from our viewpoint, this appears to be totally contradictory. Well, if you analyze cow excrement, you will find that it possesses great antiseptic qualities.
> *Katowski:* Oh, I didn't know that.
> *Prabhupada:* Dr. Ghosh, a physician, has analyzed it and has been able to prove its marvelous properties. Veda prescriptions may seem contradictory at times, but close examination will always show their exactness.

5. *Ibid.,* p. 45.

Katowski: A good method, indeed, that of accepting a viewpoint after analyzing it scientifically.[6]

The Scientology Church proposes a new method, whereby a better world can be attained, based on the "modern science of mental health" or dianetics. This is an admixture of psychological and psychoanalytical techniques—including elements of esoteric, Hinduist and Buddhist origin—sustaining that the soul is immortal and undergoes several processes of reincarnation. It offers—at a high price—therapy techniques by means of a mysterious machine called the *Hubbard-Electro-Metro-Mark V,* a machine invented by the American Church founder, L. Ron Hubbard, who lived aboard his yacht (the *Apollo*) surrounded by his closest disciples.

Of all the above-mentioned methods available, Transcendental Meditation has perhaps been most successful in fusing marginal elements with the bourgeois ambitions of the silent majority. This method is also a clear symptom of the decay of traditional liberal values at the heart of the "middle class." Benjamin Franklin's advice regarding the organization and order of everyday life means very little now to many families immersed in the extreme tensions of modern life. People nowadays turn to the East in the hopes of finding inner peace and quiet fundamentals for coping with a generalized neurosis. The great champion of Transcendental Meditation, the Maharishi Mahesh Yogi, claims to be the receptor of the teachings of his master, guru Devi; his system is to persuade men to meditate twice a day so they may "become submerged in their profound *Ego* and, beyond that, as far as the Absolute." Each candidate is assigned a personal *mantra,* a Sanskrit word meaning instrument or utensil. Its root is *man* and it is related to mental activity. Anyone practicing this technique must meditate on his *mantra* for twenty minutes every morning and evening. Transcendental Meditation is regarded as both a psychotherapeutic technique and a kind of prayer, quite adaptable to any ideology, religious or not. This technique apparently has a million followers, half of whom live in the United States; it has been used by hippies and businessmen, by some religious orders and at West Point, in prisons and at universities.

6. *Conscience and Revolution,* pamphlet quoted by Woodrow, *Les nouvelles sectes, ibid.* pp. 56–57.

Most of these sects provide a model of daily communitarian life which, according to the case, is implemented with greater or lesser severity. Long-standing sects are governed by a Puritan-type model in which the faithful have a place within a vast flock based on the traditional family unity and governed by "honesty," "work," "morals," "patriotism," the practice of "ritual prohibitions" (smoking, drinking, certain foods), the "fight against sin," "hygiene," and so on. Communitarian life becomes a *congregation* of sorts, centered on the cult of sacred texts, on knowledge regarding the revelations of their superiors, visionaries and founders, and on intense missionary and proselytizing activity. In modern sects, however, the traditional family substitution is put into practice through the establishment of a communal way of life—either inspired in hippie subculture, missionary type colonies, or monastic–type seclusion (*ashrams,* for instance). These communal groups are inserted within a large congregation or family, almost invariably governed with great authoritarianism. Their development is analogous to that of real or imaginary marginal terrorist groups. Religious and esoteric marginalism also seems to escape the dominant logic; it creates a hallucinatory spectacle, operates in a world which for the majority is opaque and incomprehensible, and creates, moreover, a simulacrum whereby "good families" converge around secure and normal mass society institutions. Like the marginal terrorist, however, the religious marginal is often an "abnormal" projection or extension of the bourgeois and petty bourgeois universe to the realm of an anti-bourgeois world. Mormons, Jehovah's Witnesses and Adventists, for instance, seem to be no more than religious versions of a flawed Borg method which, instead of heading towards the happy ideal of the integrated normal-man, has transferred this normality monster to the marginal context peopled by apocalyptic ghosts. Moon's sect and those who worship Krishna, Scientology, the Jesus Revolution, or the guru Maharaj Ji, are clearly the result of the erosion, decadence, dissolution, crisis and proletarianization of the so-called middle classes. They are all heading towards that road to Kathmandu which I have termed bourgeois proletarianization.

VII The Chariot of the Silent Majority

(The Chariot)

He called in a powerful voice to the four angels whose duty was to devastate land and sea, "Wait before you do any damage on land or at sea or to the trees, until we have put the seal on the foreheads of the servants of our God." . . . After that I saw a huge number, impossible to count, of people from every nation, race, tribe and language; they were standing in front of the throne and in front of the Lamb.

Rev. 7:2–3 and 9

On January 17, 1976, French television cameras were ready before a Saint-Germain-au-Mont-d'Or house, owned by the Moon sect and home of one of his "families." Millions avidly watched their T.V. screens as the family members of 22-year-old Marie-Christine, a teacher for maladjusted children, attempted to "rescue" the girl from the claws of the sect. The mother's attempt at persuading the girl to abandon the sect was ineffective, so the family members tried taking her away by force, convinced she had gone mad and had been "brainwashed." The silent mass of TV watchers witnessed a touching struggle between Marie-Christine's family and the wicked sect. In the end, the family took her away.

The very next day, however, Marie-Christine returned to the sect house after explaining to her family: "You don't understand. I've found the truth. I've got a purpose, which is to work, study and love my neighbor. I've got an ideal, which is to join the great perfect family."

What makes this an interesting episode is its insertion in an imagery stimulation process—diametrically opposed to the marginal imagery process—that nurtures the idea of the silent majority. The marginal problematique is, quite obviously, entirely immersed in a flux-reflux area that also embraces the opposite pole, which is to say the normal mass that claims as its heroes those hard-working and honest parents striving for liberal and comfortable happiness. The marginal cannot exist without the silent majority and vice versa; both concepts and mythologies are inexorably linked by means of a complex network of symbiotic ties.

Normal-men fighting against marginals and sects use the protection and support of the silent majority who abandon their supposed indifference. This is how all kinds of parent organizations come into being, determined to defend "individual and family values" against sects that "destroy personality," assault the individual's "psychic integrity," destroy the family and create instability within society.[1] Associations such as these join a range of existing organizations created to brave those "dangers" threatening society, such as communism, sexual perversion, drugs and suicide. What we have here, in fact, is a reproduction of sects related to the integrated normal-man's "altruistic" goals, which is to say associations for the protection of animals, the aged, the poor, the disabled and mutilated, the blind, hungry third world children, the environment, forests, people suffering from cancer, alcoholics, and so on. Thus an interesting classification of abnormal and marginal phenomena is made, so that two kinds of marginals are distinguished: those which must be *protected* and those which it becomes paramount to *attack*. Associations protecting abnormal elements marginated by "natural" processes and catastrophes (hunger, illness, war, pollution, accidents, old age) differ from associations fighting against marginals that embody the "criminal," "antisocial," "unnatural" objectives of the enemy. The question is, which enemy? Taken to extremes, this would obviously be the class enemy; although the latter is embodied in "foreign powers," "criminals," "terrorists," "subversive forces," or whatever.

When a horrified bourgeoisie realizes, however, that these marginal and criminal phenomena include their children, employees, and intellectuals—the "middle class"—they must provide an explanation that may reasonably elucidate the external and alien character of this danger, that will mark the limits of the phenomenon in the same way a crime is only really defined when the criminal is literally behind bars. While the criminal remains at large, and until the latter is recognized and captured, anyone could turn out be the guilty party, no matter to what social class he belongs; it might be a neighbor, a friend, a colleague or even a member of the family. The problem arising when bourgeois or petty bourgeois offspring become hippies, form part of esoteric sects or become militants in a

---

1. During the last years, several such associations have flourished in France: ADFI (Association for the Defense of Family and Individual Values), USIF (Union for the Safeguard of the Individual and the Family), APEDIF (Association for the Protection and Defense of the Individual and the Family), ASOFIS (Association for the Safeguard and Orientation of the Family, the Individual and Society). There are similar organizations in the United States: Save Our Children (SOC) and Americans United for Life (AUL).

left-wing political group (potentially a terrorist one), is that it is a free individual decision in which no law is flouted. No existing code forbids declassment, margination, ideological mutation, or degradation of bourgeois values. . . .

Once these associations in charge of defending the individual, family and society realize the impotence of the legal and police force apparatus, an explanation is devised. Accordingly, there are, on one hand, methods and techniques which endeavor to achieve normal-man characteristics, such as happiness, stability and integration (practical psychology methods identical to those prescribed in manuals on how to be a good salesman or businessman, or to techniques on how to become wealthy in a few weeks); there are, on the other hand, personality-destroying techniques that use destructuring—restructuring processes in minds subjected to an *external influence.* This is the celebrated "brainwashing" (called "psychic rape" in France), that old battle horse dating back to the Korean war period. The "brainwashing" myth abounds in "scientific" studies and centers on the fact that the destruction of an individual's critical sense (the famous "common sense" of the silent majority) can be induced by subjecting him to situations of great muscular fatigue, lack of sleep, inanition and isolation. It is feasible that in such conditions any ideas or information insistently and repeatedly drilled into an individual will turn even a strong-willed person into a being entirely subordinated and manipulated by another.[2] In fact, "brainwashing" amounts to little more than what the ruling class does, year in year out, to the exploited and consumer mass, as Vance Packard describes and analyzes admirably in *The Hidden Persuaders.*[3] But "brainwashing" concentrates its palpable effects in few weeks rather than many years, on the individual rather than the mass, as well as on the dominator or propitiator of domination rather than on the dominated. The discovery of sophisticated methods and advanced techniques that may lead to stability and success is counteracted by the "enemy's" discovery of specialized techniques which swiftly destabilize the normal individual—whose "normality," it turns out, is

---

2. See William Sargent, *Battle for the Mind, a Physiology of Conversion and Brain-washing,* New York: Perennial Library, 1957.
3. Vance Packard, *The Hidden Persuaders,* New York: David McKay, 1957.

purely imaginary, an invention begotten by the delimitations of marginality itself. Society thus becomes a battlefield where a contradictory compound of sects, groups and associations wage a war by means of technological-religious paraphernalia: brainwashing, exorcism, propaganda, meditation and health cures.

The actual political-cultural battleground is more like a continuous chain of everyday phenomena that join warring marginal and silent majority poles. Parent and businessmen associations are entwined with "tolerated" sects that have infiltrated bourgeois life for some time now (Masons, Rosicrucians); while altruistic charity activities are being organized at bridge parties, eccentric yet accepted therapies are being practiced, and esoteric activities fostered—all of which are considered harmless or even interesting, such as parapsychology, astrology and occultism. The generation of parents that believed in men from outer space, imagined or actually saw flying saucers, were intrigued by witch-doctors and drank a great deal of alcohol; their offspring now adore gurus, practice Transcendental Meditation, preach the arrival of the Judgment Day, and take hallucinogens or cocaine. A clear illustration of this appears in popular literature, where marginal heroes (guerrillas, eccentric sages, criminals) are locked in an endless battle against silent majority heroes (spies, agents, police, superheroes); their weapons are projections of the prototypical image of marginal activity (suffering, torture, explosives, karate, judo) and normal activity (computers, sophisticated techniques, laser beams, gadget-weapons). In popular literature, as in daily life, however, images are inverted and roles dislocated. This means that the marginal comes to possess sophisticated modern war technocracy (complex brainwashing machines, ultra-modern communication systems), whereas the superagent uses the mass-appealing exotic secrets of ancient eastern martial arts. The political rules governing this battle are not rooted in the political system's traditional logic. A clear example is that Moon's closest collaborator is an ex-military attaché of the Korean Embassy in Washington, a colonel closely linked to the CIA and head of Radio Free Asia, an anticommunist broadcasting network financed and controlled by the CIA. The Children of God who preach the Jesus Revolution, however, find allies in the third world; for them Muammar al-Qaddafi (Libya's Revolutionary Council President) is "the third world's most distinguished voice and mentor," and they accordingly see him as a "contemporary Aladdin with an oil lamp" who will show us "a third direction that will elude materialist capitalism and communist atheism."

The closely-knit mesh of marginals and the silent majority is compounded by a confused and contradictory admixture of situations relatively independent from the actual state apparatus[4] and which, on the whole, elude the control of institutions traditionally seen as the State's civil foundation—institutions such as the dominant Church, the schooling system, the family, justice and the trade unions, in addition to the political, mass-media and cultural systems. This is not to say that the marginal-silent majority duality from which the mediating mesh is created can be found in an area *differing* from that of the State apparatus; it is, in fact, composed of the very same elements. This mediating mesh, however, operates under quite different conditions and rules. As I mentioned above, the new sects, unlike the older ones, are infused with novel elements that have their origins in problems outside the traditional democratic domain, and that can be summed up as follows: consumer society is confronted, not by a redistributive consciousness, but by a religious mysticism and ceremonialism able to substitute everyday frustrations; the eastern world is embraced as an alternative to western capitalist pragmatism; and there is an indifference towards any representative, parliamentary and protectionist political apparatus and a preference for corporative organization.

The same occurs with the silent majority. In this case, the processes of political representation and the expression of sectorial interests are of no consequence. The State apparatus is based on representation and interest-channelling mechanisms which presuppose the existence of a social class system. This is to say that school provides the system's elemental rules, the family provides a direction for these efforts, justice ensures a "fair" distribution of the interests of all concerned, the predominant church represents God, unions represent professional groups, mass media steer the diversity of opinions, the political system sanctions the representation of all

---

4. These escape because they partly operate at an international and transnational scale, whereas the majority of State apparatuses operate within the limits of national boundaries.

parties, and the cultural system provides entertainment even as it fulfills a role of persuasion for each social segment.

Yet this new social substance or silent majority cannot be poured into the waterways of the State apparatus. The silent majority lives in a homogeneous world governed by theatrical rites and ceremonies, techniques of persuasion, in addition to social mutation signs and signals. It is a world in which *representation or the expression of interests* gives way entirely to the practice of techniques that may lead to success or happiness, which, in turn, will purportedly reveal the secret of the normal-man model—a model that is, after all, only the petty bourgeois imaginary projection of a stereotyped ruling class.

The new precepts of modern social imagery are established through the opposition of democratic-liberal dynamics; this is to say that the silence of the majority is nurtured by the spectacular noise of the marginal minorities, whereas the latter justify their actions in the silence of the masses. The terrorist act and the sermons of religious or secular sects seek to arouse mass awareness, although this merely increases its muteness. And it is this very muteness and indifference that stimulates desperate acts and mystical escapism. Whereas marginals inhabit a world where destiny is continually postponed, the silent majority is experiencing a premature destiny. Marginals make sacrifices today so they may invoke an everpostponed destiny; they pay today so they may travel tomorrow. Inversely, the silent majority travels today and pays later—as the publicity fostered by credit institutions proclaims.

This diabolical vicious circle—by means of which the bourgeois define normality using marginal segments as a reference point, while abnormal fractions are regarded as deviations from the norm—is based on a series of ideas and actions apparently detached from the State apparatus. Yet this provides the State with the indispensable aura of legitimacy created by the silent approval of the majority. This phenomenon is different from propaganda or amusement (TV and sports are obvious examples). The latter tend to contrive a deception and waylay consciousness; they are the old, well-known complement to bread handed out to the populace, which is to say the *circuses*. Inversely, the mediating imagery that proceeds from the *marginal-majority* dialectic is nevertheless based on a group of objective social movements and actions all of which share the characteristic of being class struggle *fragments*. The majority that rides the silence-legitimizing chariot does not ride out of entertainment or conviction (in other words, because football is more interesting or because they are swayed by the predominant propaganda). If the so-called silent majority is to become effective, it must also be part of a set of real struggle, success and defeat fragments. The problem is to ascertain exactly how their fragmentation came about and how they came to be ordered in such a way that their very presence induces major mediating results.

VIII The Balance between Democracy and Marginality

(Justice)

The seven angels that had the seven trumpets now made ready to sound them.

Rev. 8:6

It might prove interesting to follow a different path now in discussing subjacent ideas in previous chapters. These ideas can be simplified and summarized as follows: modern capitalist societies undergo important non-democratic processes that provide political legitimacy, operate in the realm of the *marginality-silent majority* flux, and have no norms, typical of the liberal tradition, that derive from State apparatuses (whether repressive or ideological).

I have borrowed from mainstream American sociology the alternative route I am proposing to follow, in an attempt to prove that not only does a political process exist continually regenerating these non-democratic mediation structures, but that its expansion constitutes a political plan contemplated by important sectors of the American State.

Let us take a look at the mechanism of a (simplified) simulation model—based on the theory of games—which may corroborate Tocqueville's famous paradigm: *the greater the democracy and equality, the lesser the legitimacy of the political system.*[1] Let us suppose we have a social group of 20 people simulating a society and that each is asked to make a voluntary contribution of a dollar so that five may be won at a game of chance (a lottery); since there can only be five winners, the probability of winning diminishes as the number of players increases. If only five people play, they will all win; if 16 people play, eleven will lose. Let us try to foresee the outcome—particularly the degree of frustration a game such as this would provoke. Each player's probabilities are as follows:

1. This model was originally designed by Samuel A. Stoufer, *The American Soldier*, Princeton, N.J.: Princeton University Press, 1949. See Comments by Raymond Boudon, *Effets Pervers et Ordre Social*, Paris: PUF, 1977.

a) If only five people play, each is sure to win four dollars (five dollars minus the one they invested).

b) If six people play, one of them will lose a dollar, which is to say that each has five probabilities in six of winning; mathematically, the probability of each is $(5/6) \times (4) + (1/6) \times (-1) = 3.2$. This is to say, five probabilities in six of winning four dollars as opposed to one probability in six of losing a dollar. Chances of winning are positive, which means playing is worthwhile.

c) If seven people play, their probabilities are as follows: $(5/7) \times (4) + (2/7) \times (-1) = 2.6$. Chances of winning are still fair.

d) The greater the number of players in the game, the less chances each has of winning. If all 20 play, the chances each has of winning become $(5/20) \times (4) + (15/20) \times (-1) = 0.25$. The chances are quite low, although still positive.

Let us imagine that according to the social norms of this group it is reasonable to participate so long as there is a positive chance of winning. What is the outcome of this competitive structure? All will invest a dollar, five will win and 15 will lose; we could then say that 75 percent of these people will feel dissatisfied and frustrated.

Let us now suppose that the dictator governing the destinies of this little social group decides—as a means of contending with the complaints of the majority—to have two winners instead of five. The outcome of this undemocratic restriction concerning the player's possibilities of winning will then be as follows:

a) The likelihood of winning remains positive if less than ten players participate. If three people play we will have $(2/3) \times (4) + (1/3) \times (-1) = 2.3$. If ten people play the chances are $(2/10) \times (4) + (8/10) \times (-1) = 0$.

b) If more than ten players participate, the chances are negative. The chances of 15 players will be $(2/15) \times (4) + (13/15) \times (-1) = -0.33$. If all 20 play the chances will be $(2/20) \times (4) + (18/20) \times (-1) = -0.5$.

If we assume no one can possibly know what decisions the others will take, every person will reason in the same way: "if I start out by assuming that the majority will participate, then it would be better not to play; although the others may think the same as me. If, however, I start out by assuming that the majority will not play, then it is in my interest to play; although if all the others reason as I do, they will then participate and the chances of winning will become negative. . . ." Let us suppose that the reasonable way out of this problem is that each decides at random their participation in the lottery, so that half the people invest a dollar and the other half do not.

The outcome would be two happy winners, eight dissatisfied or frustrated losers and ten relatively indifferent people who did not play. It becomes clear that the decrease in the probabilities of winning provokes a lesser degree of frustration (40 percent dissatisfied players). In other words, greater redistribution of profits provokes greater frustration; the more equality there is, the greater the dissatisfaction. Further sophistication in the development of this model will naturally lead to the very threshold of the relationship between the number of winners and the rate of frustration; if we were to introduce more factors the outcome would be different and so varied that we could use them to prove almost any thesis.[2] I have no interest, however, in making a critical appraisal of the theory of games as applied to sociology.

What I wish to underline here is that the key to the game lies in the increase or decrease in the number of people who decide not to play—which is to say the importance of *marginality* and *silence* in a section of society—and the assumption that this depends on the greater or lesser degree of democracy that exists in the rules of the game.

Let us now take another example, this time from a "game" far closer to political power. A report handed in to the Trilateral Commission by Samuel P. Huntington—an outstanding sociologist and

---

2. When he developed the model, Raymond Boudon (*Effets Pervers*), for instance, went as far as saying that "when the number of winners exceeds 10 or 20 percent, the rate of frustration goes from 70 to 80 percent; but when the number of winners exceeds 20 to 30 percent, the rate of frustration descends from 80 to 70 percent. If this result is combined with the effect of a decrease or increase in the inequality of possibilities, one can see that all possible cases can, in theory, be observed. In other words, an increase in the number of winners or, to move on to the language of games and that of sociology, *an increase in social mobility can coincide either with an increase or a decrease of the level of global frustration,*" p. 153. Emphasis added.

advisor to the Carter government—reveals a thought process analogous to the simulation model described above. It is worth expounding on as it represents a major political alternative presented to the United States, a country where democracy tends to become "ungovernable."[3]

Huntington's central thesis is the following: *"The vitality of democracy in the United States during the 1960's produced a substantial increase in governmental activity and a substantial decrease in governmental authority."*[4] "Vitality of democracy" means, in fact, an important increase in political and social struggle centered on three main axes: a) "social issues, such as the use of drugs, civil liberties and the role of women"; b) "racial issues, involving integration, busing, government aid to minority groups and urban riots"; c) "military issues, involving primarily, of course, the war in Vietnam, but also the draft, military spending, military aid programs and the role of the military-industrial complex more generally."[5]

The rise of popular struggle during the sixties was translated into the expansion of the State's functions in civil economy (welfare) and in the military field (repression)—what Huntington termed "an increase of governmental activity." Actually, and as a means of contending with increasing demands and pressures, State expenditure in 1974 was as much as 33 percent of the Gross National Product, which caused inflation to rocket and was like adding fuel to the flames of the social conflicts. All this cost the American State a great loss of legitimacy and a certain disintegration (readjustment, in fact) of the government coalition consolidated at the end of the Second World War. Huntington defines this government coalition as "the president acting with the support and cooperation of key individuals and groups in the Executive Office, the federal bureaucracy, Congress, and the more important businesses, banks, law firms, foundations and media, which constitute the private establishment."[6]

The deterioration of state legitimacy reached its peak during

---

3. "The United States," by S. P. Huntington, in *The Crisis of Democracy: Report on the Governability of Democracies to the Trilateral Commission*, by Michael J. Crozier, Samuel P. Huntington and Joji Watanuki, New York: New York University Press, 1975.
4. *Ibid.*, p. 64.
5. *Ibid.*, p. 77.
6. *Ibid.*, p. 92.

the Watergate scandal. The Presidency's power waned when confronted with mass media and Congress.[7] The remedy for this loss of legitimacy was—closely resembling the simulation game in this sense—that democracy be curbed, since State authority problems supposedly stem from an "excess of democracy." This means that authority elements pertaining to the government apparatus must be strengthened. What is more—and this is the same conclusion as regards the game theory—Huntington claims that

> the effective operation of a democratic political system usually requires some measure of *apathy and noninvolvement* on the part of some individuals and groups. In the past, every democratic society has had a *marginal population,* of greater or lesser size, which has not actively participated in politics. In itself, *the marginality on the part of certain groups is inherently undemocratic, but it has also been one of the factors which has enabled democracy to function effectively.* Marginal social groups, as in the case of the blacks, are now becoming full participants in the political system. Yet the danger of overloading the political system with demands which extend its functions and undermine its authority still remains. Less marginality on the part of some groups thus needs to be replaced by more self-restraint on the part of all groups.[8]

The actual political project that characterizes "postindustrial" society is far more complex than Huntington's crude statements would lead us to believe. The problem is how, and by what means, to substitute traditional democratic-parliamentary mechanisms? The answer lies in the fact that *marginality* fulfills this *function*—a statement which obviously cancels the "marginal" nature of the marginals themselves, since they are given the specific and central function of lending legitimacy to the system. Such is the strategy of

---

7. Huntington, *Crisis of Democracy,* introduces an abusive but highly symptomatic idea: "There are certain parallels between Congress and European communist parties, as described by Michael Crozier. One and the other have become for some time used to carry out opposition rules; in declining power and the authority of other groups, the power of these two institutions (mass media and Congress) grows; and a crucial question for the future—and the governability—of democracy in France, Italy and the United States, is whether these opposition bodies can adapt to fulfill government responsibility roles. It turns out that professor Crozier is a little more optimistic about the European communist parties, than I as regards the United States Congress at this moment," *Crisis of Democracy,* p. 102n.

8. *Ibid.,* p. 114.

the so-called "new politics";[9] their basic proposal concerns the problem of how to transform these new forms of struggle and dissatisfaction into something functional regarding the survival of the new
postindustrial and postdemocratic social order. It is an attempt to
transform social struggle into *dissidence*—which is to say marginality. This presupposes that the struggle based on classes, or even
professional, social segments is disappearing to give way to protest
groups (students and minorities) that conform "new life-style subcultures," distinguished by the fact they cut across ethnic and class
borderlines. These "subcultures" operate in a similar way to the new
religious sects. According to the new politics, such forms of dissidence entail a "new individualism" that traditional political fields
are unable to absorb or control; since economic coercion fails to
operate when confronted with generalized indifference, a context is
created—so we are told—which favors "mobilization politics" and
substitutes "pluralist elitism" and "traditional liberalism," both of
which have found repression as the only means of solving social
conflicts. Thus, the political activity front is shifted from the execu-
tive-legislative level to the administrative one. This resource redistribution is taken over by administration offices in terms of the new
life-style subcultures rather than in terms of social classes; this also
means that the different life-styles will create "mobilized political
groups" that will exert pressure on the administrative system, thus
enabling legislative and executive powers to act with greater freedom. According to new politics treatise writers, these ideas have
already been accepted in "post-welfare society" by women's and gay
liberation movements, both of which are regarded as examples of the
new subcultures. Thus the "new politics" model will make the class
struggle cancellation dream come true!

A British author who shares these ideas has stated that the new
model is one of "collaboration-consensus" and should prepare itself
to absorb diversity and dissidence. It will, moreover, foster the latter so as to assess people's predisposition towards it and find means
of adapting itself to the situation. It will foster the "creative disor-

---

9. Orion White, Jr., and Gideon Sjoberg, "The Emerging 'New Politics' in America," in
Politics in the Post-Welfare State, (Ed. by M. Donald Hancock and Gideon Sjoberg), New
York: Columbia University Press, 1972.

der" of a "new class whose most valued property is what they carry in their heads" and which will mobilize the new politics—"action politics"—impelled by "unmarried mothers, the handicapped, immigrants and those in poverty."[10] This will not become, however, an anarchic dissidence, but one that offers forms of struggle in which *efficiency* and *participation* coverage, giving way to a "technology of social rebellion"; this is to say a domesticated form of rebellion under State service, a rebellion of efficient marginals before which the traditional bureaucratic system will prove flexible by allowing groups and subgroups to organize self-administration forms in accordance with the dominant system and with the flux and reflux of new pressure forms. What we have here, in fact, is the bureaucratization of civil society and the civilization of the political-administrative apparatus. Sjoberg and White have stated the following:

> Forms of influence and pressure tactics as overcompliance with administrative rules, paracompliance, and the guerrilla theater will become legitimized. The citizenry will likely build upon some of the strategies that have delegitimized traditional authority systems as a means of sustaining a greater responsiveness to the electorate on the part of those who command positions of power.[11]

Here we have, then, the guerilla theater, the simulation model where all these sects—either parareligious, new philosophers, dissidents, prisoners, immigrant minorities, homosexuals, hippies, feminists, or anything bearing the "marginal" label (whether as a deviation from the norm or as a silent and indifferent minority)—are parts belonging to a democratic-parliamentary mechanism gradually substituted by a mediating administrative system both tolerant and flexible. Tolerant, of course, towards "marginal" class contradictions expressions, though inflexible and despotic towards "older" and "old-fashioned" social conflicts. It is a model that seems to wish the class contradictions were concealed under the mantle of a classless, pluralist and decentralized society, a mantle woven from class struggle refuse, fragmented into subcultures and life-styles. The

---

10. Douglas L. Capps, "The Citizen, Administration and Politics in Post-Welfare Britain," in *Politics in the Post-Welfare State*, pp. 176ff.
11. Sjoberg and White, *Politics*, p. 28.

State thereby seats itself all the more comfortably at the center, concentrating even more power, without having to practice centralist politics; democracy stands in the way of the State, as once the former ceases to be useful in curbing popular pressures, the State must intervene by using centralist and repressive means to prevent these pressures from overflowing. The game theory, the Trilateral Commission thesis and the "new politics" are trumpet calls announcing the destruction of liberal pagan civil society, dominated by the demons of democracy.

IX Through the Looking-Glass

(The Hermit)

They were forbidden to harm any fields or crops or trees and told only to attack any men who were without God's seal on their foreheads.

Rev. 9:4

Among the many functions the modern capitalist State must fulfill is the regulation of marginal conditions pertaining to the production process. This is to say that the State intervenes in the economy not as a government apparatus acting as an additional capitalist enterprise, but in terms of an action with specific characteristics, an action engendering the illusion of a State that socially regulates the collective welfare, and attacks and represses only those enemies who do not bear the legitimizing seal of the political apparatus.[1]

The capitalist structure itself, however, cultivates these potential enemies; the labor market cannot operate without constantly maintaining a permanent unemployed mass, without an industrial army in reserve. The contradiction lies in the fact that this mass must be educated and trained so it may eventually fulfill its function as a reserve, although there is a simultaneous need to maintain it *outside capitalist production,* which is done by educating it as a proletariat but keeping it from working in the factory. Suzanne de Brunhoff points out that "it is here where *non-capitalist institutions*— with State-like attributes to a greater or lesser extent—intervene to ensure the reproduction of the labor force within those limits by means of which the fundamental insecurity regarding employment is maintained, and within those forms which guarantee that work discipline is maintained."[2] These institutions—ranging from primitive bourgeois institutions in aid of the poor to modern social security systems—not only fulfill a fundamental economic function, but

1. On the marginal conditions of the productive process, see Joachim Hirsch, "Remarques théoriques sur l'Etat bourgeois et sa crise," in *La crise de l'Etat,* edited by N. Poulantzas, Paris: Presses Universitaires de France, 1976. Regarding the illusion of the social state, see Wolfgang Müller and Chris Neusüss, "The 'Welfare-State Illusion' and the Contradiction between Wage Labor and Capital," in *State and Capital,* edited by J. Halloway & Picciotto, London: Arnold, 1978.
2. *Etat et Capital,* Grenoble: Presses Universitaires de Grenoble, 1976, p.8. Emphasis added.

also trace the solid nucleus on which most of the capitalist exploitation's legitimizing imagery depends.

The economic function of these institutions is fundamental, since the State apparatus organizes the payment of complementary "wages" (by means of services) indispensable for the reproduction of the labor force *as a whole*. The private capitalist pays wages that correspond to the "daily value" of the labor force, but which do not ensure its "reproduction value." In other words, the private capitalist pays neither (or only partially) for the support of children, the diseased, the unemployed, nor for the education (and repression) expenses of all those "marginals." The State organizes and oversees the global process of the labor force reproduction and carefully ensures that the mass of women, children, aged, diseased and unemployed is sealed by the blessings of social security, public health and schooling, even though it is "non-productive."

In fact, the State apparatus tends to intervene prominently (and to a greater extent during crises) in every economic activity the private capitalist finds unattractive. Whenever production time is prolonged or profits are uncertain, or else products are not destined for immediate consumption, there is no profitability or only a low one, the initial capital is too large for a single enterprise—in all these instances the State intervenes as an ideal global capitalist, as Engels would say. These realms of State investment are, however, fundamental, such as education, scientific research, communication systems, public health, social security, water distribution, energy production, urban garbage collection, and so on. The State appears in all these as a non-capitalist process within a capitalist context; it is in charge of ensuring the development of non-capitalist mechanisms indispensable for the reproduction of the capitalist system as a whole. Elmar Altvater has carefully studied the ways in which the modern State takes on responsibility for non-profit production that cannot be carried out on a capitalist basis; he concludes that "the State is a non-capitalist element within a capitalist society, although, on the other hand, it is a capitalist with full rights whose expenditure is invested in a capitalist kind of production."[3] This

---

3. E. Altvater, "Remarques sur quelques problèmes posés par l'interventionisme étatique," in *L'Etat contemporain et le Marxisme*, Paris: Maspero, 1975, p. 142.

process occurs most clearly when the State intervenes in the agriculture of so-called underdeveloped countries undergoing agrarian reforms;[4] the State evidently takes over not only the organization of the most modern *non-capitalist* processes, but also—and during precise historical periods—the control (and thus the destruction simultaneous to the refunctionalization) of *precapitalist* elements. It is precisely during the period of primitive capital accumulation that the State acquires its modern form. This is why I believe that the State's set of non-capitalist activities can be defined as a process of *permanent primitive accumulation.*

What I wish to underline is that what has been defined as monopolistic State capitalism has specific characteristics of its own; it is not merely the development of a capitalist super-enterprise— larger than any other and headed by the government—but the growth of a vast group of activities and services that are not directly or immediately productive and which involve a wage-earning mass defined by its position within political force correlations rather than by its immersion in economic mechanisms of accumulation.[5] Regarding the above-mentioned, it has justifiably been asserted that the growth of wage-earning labor within the State apparatus is an expansion of the exploitation of the *concrete use value* of work and not of its *abstract use value* (aimed at generating surplus value). This new situation, which acquires massive proportions, indicates the existence of non-capitalist dynamics that extend to a population section which has little to do with the imperatives of a specifically capitalist labor force value (such as employees, bureaucrats, and salaried professionals).[6]

This vast group of State mechanisms nurtures three different parts of the population:

 a) Those who are wage-earners but not directly productive or are inserted within productive processes where profits are either "socialized" or low, or else engendered only on a

4. On the non-capitalist character of agriculture fostered by the State, see Roger Bartra, *Estructura agraria y clases sociales en Mexico,* Mexico: Ediciones Era, 1974. (Translated in Roger Bartra, *Peasantry and Capitalism,* Baltimore: Johns Hopkins University Press, forthcoming.)

5. See Vincent's interesting article, "L'Etat en crise," *La crise de l'Etat.*

6. Claus Offe, *Strukturprobleme des kapitalistischen Staates,* Frankfurt, 1972.

long-term basis. This is where we find the ill-assorted political bureaucracy, wage-earners in State or semi-independent government agency services, technocracy, intellectuals and teachers.

b) The non-productive and relatively inactive "marginal" population, maintained so that the labor force as a whole can be reproduced, such as the unemployed, retired and diseased, as well as children, youth and students. This population is also connected with what is called the "second economy" or "informal sector."

c) The traditional petty bourgeoisie protected by the State apparatus, since it ensures certain services or products not easily centralized (such as restaurants, small businesses, arts and crafts, certain agricultural products) and whose downfall could entail serious political consequences that would drive the system off-balance

These groups are thus constituted in major social sectors and appear to displace the fundamental contradiction of a capitalist society—which is to say the one that antagonistically opposes the proletariat to the bourgeoisie. I do not wish to embark here on a discussion—frequently a byzantine one—regarding the "end of class society and of ideologies." Evidently, this new situation, far from pointing to the end of social classes (particularly proletarian ones)—an event anxiously awaited by the ruling class—points to the massive irruption of social classes within the political apparatus. There can be no doubt, however, that this is a new phenomenon expressing a new condition of the class contradictions and consequently, a new expression of the social classes themselves.

The massive irruption within the State of the new social conflicts, together with the phenomenon of political apparatus extension of "civil" activities, create the illusion of socialization. This illusion—the first step through the looking-glass—corresponds to objective economic processes and depends on the degree to which the tendency towards the extinction of the State has matured, something which is, quite obviously, impossible under capitalist conditions. In most developed countries, however, the "social State" apparatus has induced authoritarian- or totalitarian-type tendencies. Thus the correlation between State monopolistic mechanisms and the new mediating political imagery becomes evident; how can one fail to see the link between the expansion of non-profitable economic activities, which are foreign to the "free" labor market, and anti-liberal political tendencies? It becomes obvious that the issues arising from the discussion about the State's extended socioeconomic functions—education, welfare, communication, energy, public health—bear a close relationship to the phenomena of marginalism, subcultures, mass media predominance, millenarianism, abnormality, and the rest. It would seem that the students were responsible, in 1968, for unleashing marginal segment ambitions; that ethnic minorities forced the extension of welfare; that the technological revolution in mass media inspired structuralist imagery; that the use of atomic energy contributed to millenarian sect development; that the extension of public health triggered abnormal segment definition. And the workers? The bourgeoisie? They seem to have vanished into a historical past, to have become ancient history altogether buried by a new postindustrial society made up of techno-structures, intellectuals, employees, bureaucrats, marginals, subcultures, pressure groups.

It becomes possible to "prove" that the most important—numerically speaking—social group within areas of greater development is linked to the "services." Thanks to the classifying mechanism devised by Colin Clark several decades ago, it is possible to statistically prove that the "tertiary" (service) sector tends to be larger to the detriment of the primary (agriculture and mining) and secondary (industry) sectors. According to Daniel Bell, in 1970, 60 percent of the U.S. labor force was employed in services. Other developed countries are following the same route.[7] This is an attempt to demonstrate, among other things, the tendency towards the extinction of the proletariat within modern capitalist societies.

It is also feasible, on the other hand, to "prove" that the majority is composed of marginals. For instance, Juergen Ruesch has added up the number of physically disabled, psychiatric institution patients, individuals sought by the law, drug-addicts and alcoholics in the United States. To these he added the aged, unemployed,

---

7. Daniel Bell, *The Coming of Post-Industrial Society: A Venture in Social Forecasting,* New York: Basic Books, 1973.

mentally disabled, chronically diseased, individuals in rehabili-
tation, and so on. All these amounted to 30 percent of the U.S.
adult population in 1965. The same author calculated that only 35
percent of the population fulfills a function; taking minors into account—and added to the above-mentioned marginals—the results
indicate that 65 percent of the American population is marginal.
This author's description and codification of modern society is solid
and succinct when he states with utmost conviction that

> In a classless postindustrial society, social mobility is based on
> horizontal movements that enable the access or exit from the
> power structure. Modern population is thereby formed by a
> central group (10 percent) which embraces government, in-
> dustry, finance, science, engineering, the army and education.
> Around this center revolves a circle of goods and service con-
> sumers, organized by those at the center (25 percent). On the
> fringe are the marginals (65 percent) who have no significant
> function in our society.[8]

If one adds to this illusion the confirmation that on a world
scale—and particularly in the third world—this population is de-
voted predominantly to agriculture (over 58 percent of world labor
force in 1967), history seems to leave no more than a narrow space
for the industrial proletariat, situated amid a world of peasants,
wage-earners and marginals. To make matters worse, that multitude
depends to a greater or lesser extent on the State—as was discussed
above—which means the proletariat is almost reduced to the condition of a hermit, a historical character, invented by Karl Marx in
the 19th century, who lives outside the universe of the new political
structure of the so-called postindustrial society.

It is clear that the logical basis of this sociological imagery is
formed by a previous classification exercise. Interpretations such as
these can be made thanks to a lever which, in turn, provides a
support constituted by functionalist-inspired analytical-classifying
systems; once the latter are built, they allow for the empirical de-
tection of social structures which are adaptable to the interests of

---

8. Juergen Ruesch, "Social Disability: The Problem of Misfits in Society," paper read for
"Towards a Healthy Community" Congress, (World Federation for Mental Health and Social
Psychiatry), Edinburgh, May 1969.

those who "discover" them. Thus the new sociologist can exclaim: allow me to classify and I will raise the world!

These manipulations should not prevent us, however, from losing sight of something vitally important; namely, that the changes in the population's constitution in advanced capitalist societies—changes reflected even in the most primitive statistic-classifying methods—indicate the presence of new tendencies at the core of the State apparatus. These new tendencies emerge particularly in what is termed the *expansion of the State's social and economic apparatuses and activities*. I have already briefly pointed out that this kind of activity constitutes an extension of "ideal global capitalist" functions. These activities are chiefly guided towards four separate directions:

a) The control, centralization and activation, under a monopolistic guise, of not strictly capitalist State and semi-independent government agency processes (for instance communication system construction, technical scientific research, energy generation and distribution). These processes generate a mass of wage-earners and technocrats of different levels, who are mostly an extension of the working class under new forms within the State.

b) The organization of conditions vital for the reproduction of the labor force as a whole (public health, social security, universities, schools). Also related to these activities is a mass of employees in which a significant intellectual sector is included. Moreover, the very nature of these activities ensures their continual contact with the population's "marginal" sectors, towards which a significant part of their action is guided (unemployed, diseased, students).

c) The protection and refunctionalization of certain non-capitalist and off-centered social and economic functions (informal activities, small-scale business, industry, and agriculture, arts and crafts); this is where the permanence of petty bourgeois social segments is stimulated and where capitalist competitive and monopolistic concentration processes—which lead to the petty bourgeoisie's downfall—are relatively controlled. Very often a particular form of monopolistic concentration at a circulation and financing level is stimulated, although this maintains the (relative) independence of small-scale producers or businessmen.

d) The reorganization of traditional political-administrative activities that enable the bureaucracy to adapt to the new control requirements of the vast State edifice.

Social mobility processes are produced within these four large areas, thereby creating the illusion that these "postindustrial" society mobility processes imply the access or exit to the power structure (that is, whether one is "in" or "out"). However, it is true that as time goes by, social mobility clearly has greater political overtones, whereas politics increasingly adopt "social" forms; this is where the new myths surrounding the State's socialization (and de-politization) and the statization of civil society have their origin. This new mythology and imagery, however, has an objective basis—namely, the expansion of the State apparatus in the above-mentioned four areas. The processes I have termed the *embourgeoisement* of the working class and the proletarianization of the bourgeoisie operate here in a spectacular way; since these processes are a combination of real and imaginary tendencies, they ensure the permanent operation of the complex apparatus of political mediation. One of the parts conforming this apparatus is the structuralist classifying method which conceptually isolates the *segments* of real processes and conflicts and establishes them as prototypical axes or characters. The following diagram represents this mediating process:

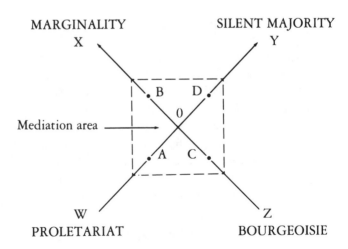

Each arrow represents, respectively, the imaginary continuation of antagonistic class ambitions and struggles (W-Y) or fears and resistances (Z-X), a continuation that extends to both prototypical extremes, that of the marginal and that of the normal-man. The W-O-Z triangle, in which two sides respectively cross points A and C, represents—so to speak—the *real social basis of social contradictions;* the latter, in other words, antagonically confront the two major social classes of our time. The upper triangle (X-O-Y) represents the *mediating apparatus,* partly inserted in the institutional solidity of the State and partly immersed in the clouds of imagination. Points A, B, C and D represent the above-defined social segments and areas of State activity (which is to say, respectively, technocrat-wage-earners, intellectual-wage-earners, petty bourgeoisie and bureaucrats). The Z-X axis, labelled the proletarianization of the bourgeoisie indicates the imaginary extension—going beyond point O and thereby reaching the extreme boundary of class enemy antagonism—of the petty bourgeoisie's real downfall and of the intellectual's proletarianization; marginality here becomes the transference to the antibourgeois world of petty bourgeois and intellectual traits. The W-Y axis of the proletarian *embourgeoisement,* however, shows in diagram form the ideal extension of the working class's "tertiary function" and of its expansion (and ascension) to the "service" sector, on its way to the antiproletarian pole where white-collar-clean-handed wage-earner traits blend with the bureaucrat's peculiarities.

Although the above diagram is a geometrical representation, it enables one to situate in a sort of theoretical geography the area I have defined as the mediating apparatus or structure. In fact, the mediation's triangular area is cut across by many axes which imaginarily continue the various aspects of the social struggle (by no means reduced to a bourgeois-proletariat antagonism) and which, as they intercross, form a dense network. The mediation world is like Wonderland through the looking-glass, which mirrors social contradictions and enables class actors to watch the spectacle of their own conflicts. Similarly to what occurs when we are facing a looking-glass—where the signs made by our right hand are mirrored by the left hand in the looking-glass image—resembling the way in which society's most numerous and silenced class appears to be a noisy marginal minority, whereas society's ruling and minority class is mirrored as the silent majority. State and power are presented here as a looking-glass in which an inverted image is mirrored, although this is by no means a clear-cut image, since modern history has covered the looking-glass surface with cracks, distortions and opacities. This State-looking-glass metaphor reflects far more accurately the actual political tendencies than the old images of the Keynesian State-vigilant or the liberal State-parliament that substituted the ideas of a State-sun shining on every individual and of the State-castle as a fortress peopled by medieval lords.

The monster that emerges, full of symbols, inventions and new words, from Wonderland through the looking-glass—a legacy of Lewis Carroll's—provides an image of the modern State which supersedes that of Leviathan. This monster is the

ЈАВВЕRWOCK

This is how it appears in Lewis Carroll's verses:

> "Twas brillig and the slithy toves
> Did gyre and gimble in the wabe:
> All mimsy were the borogoves
> And the mome raths outgrabe.
>
> "Beware the Jabberwock, my son!
> The Jaws that bite, the claws that catch!
> Beware the Jubjub bird, and shun
> The frumius Bandersnatch!"

X   The Symbiotic Structure Simulacrum

(The Wheel of Fortune)

So I took it out of the angel's hand, and swallowed it; it was sweet as honey in my mouth, but when I had eaten it my stomach turned sour. Then I was told, "You are to prophesy again, this time about many different nations and countries and languages and emperors."

Rev. 10:10–11

In one of Wilder Pembroke's classical studies which gave rise to what was later known as the symbiotic structure theory, he conclusively stated the following:

> In our research on social balance, developed from a previous conflicting situation, we have found a symbiosis between two different kinds of structures: a) those that contain *internal* dynamics of their own; thereby continually generating conditions leading to their self-extinction, disappearance, transformation and death; b) those that are created by means of *external* factors, which means they do not contain reproduction mechanisms leading to self-extinction since the impulses that determine their disappearance emerge externally. A balanced society always contains both kinds of structures. The first kind engenders the second kind as a means of postponing self-extinction; and although the second kind lacks a life of its own, its function is to prolong the life of the first. The second structure constitutes the crystallized and institutionalized death of the first; the latter constitutes the decadent and borrowed life of the former. The second kind is the present future of the first; whereas the first kind is the present past of the second kind. The first kind of structure creates the second kind, thereby producing an illusion of transcendence, although the second one actually constitutes an illusion of immanence.[1]

This description of social balance is similar to the wheel and to the salamander devouring its own tail. The structure which, according to Pembroke's definition, contains its own dynamics also contains the *symptoms of self-extinction*. What distinguishes some of these symptoms is a "displacement" of functions and social sectors towards

1. Wilder Pembroke, "A re-examination of correlations between lynchings and economic indices in heterocultural groups," in *Journal of Socially-Induced Cognitive Simulacra*, Innsmouth, Mass.: 1927, vol. XIV, n. 51, pp. 243–97.

activities and life-styles that contradict traditional internal dynamics of the social structure. This "displacement," however, conditions the development of another structure "peopled by social ghosts." Pembroke establishes an analogy—which is highly characteristic of him—with Biblical symbolism, by comparing the political beasts of the Revelation—invented as a means of stimulating the illusion of the immanence of God's kingdom on earth—with the political-ideological imagery of what I have preferred to call the mediation structure: "Just as no New Jerusalem advent can take place without the existence of Babylonia the Great, the domination of the leisure class cannot consolidate itself without evoking the demons of democracy."[2] This idea is interesting, although, like so many of Pembroke's statements, it is open to ambiguous interpretations.

A certain parallel could be established between what Pembroke defines as external-factor-determined structures that generate illusions of immanence, and those I have already defined as *mediation structures*. Actually, the ideological mediation is generated by "articulation points" between antagonistic poles or different structures. This is to say—as I have already explained—between those social groups that experience closely the borderline that separates different classes or historical periods. This borderline, however, appears as an "articulation point" between mediating State structures and the mass population (civil society). Incidentally, Nicole Thibodeaux has pointed out that "the articulation between one precapitalist mode of production and the capitalist mode of production seems to reproduce itself in the relationship between the social apparatus of monopolistic State capitalism and private civil society."[3] Although the comparison between precapitalist economy and the modern State is somewhat misapplied here (this author is obviously greatly influenced by the Italian school which considers modern society to be "neofeudal"), it is true that the articulation between the civil structure and the mediating State structure implies a "symbiosis," as Pembroke would say, between the dynamics of private capital

2. *A Structural Analysis of Conflict*, Innsmouth, Mass.: Gilman House Press, 1933, p. 271. The author never completed this book due to a serious mental derangement that began in 1928, the symptoms of which can be perceived in the book's final chapters.
3. Nicole Thibodeaux, *Simulation, stratégie et capitalisme monopolique d'Etat*, Villeurbaine: La Gaffe, 1977.

(which entails self-extinction) and the mediating social functions of the modern State (a logic that can be explained only in terms of its relationship to private capital).

Could one say—as many authors have asserted—that any situation that entails the articulation of different structures generates despotic and authoritarian tendencies? Flieger has carried out a fairly detailed analysis of transition periods and situations and claimed that "totalitarian" phenomena appear in every case: the Asiatic mode of production (oriental despotism), the transition from feudalism to capitalism (absolute monarchy), underdeveloped countries (dictatorships), the crisis-induced transition from liberal capitalism to monopolistic capitalism (fascism), the transition to socialism (Stalinism).[4] It should be added that the unexpected transition from socialism to capitalism after 1989 in Europe will possibly develop also authoritarian and nationalist tendencies (already visible in Poland). Despite the fact Flieger uses Anglo-Saxon sociological traditions related to "total power" as his starting-point, this study is highly stimulating and his hypotheses are very important. In actual fact, authoritarian processes are formed (although each is very different from the other) when there is an articulation between a structure "economically" or "naturally" reproduced and another "politically" reproduced—which is to say, when economy is dominant in one and politics in the other; as Pembroke would say, the articulation of an *immanent-structure-generating-an-illusion-of-transcendence* with another *transcendent-structure-provoking-an-illusion-of-immanence.* This means the articulation of different historical periods (or modes of production) resembles the articulation of dissimilar structural instances within that same society. However, this resemblance lacks all sense, when expressed in abstract and general terms, since any society, during any period, is in "transition" and contains differing "structural instances." The problem lies in how to locate social areas and historical periods in which the articulation is concentrated and intensified, and how to proceed from there to determine what provokes this phenomenon in each case. The two period division Flieger proposes is valid enough, although too general: a) when the natural

4. N. Flieger, *Modern and Ancient Totalitarian Models,* Middletown: Radical University Press, 1969.

community confronts the *polis;* b) when the developed *polis* (capital-ism) confronts the new community (non-capitalist, socialist mecha-nisms). An intermediate period is added in which the feudal *polis* confronts the capitalist *polis.*

From this perspective the *democratic phenomenon* would simul-taneously be a) the illusion functioning as a bridge that saves class antagonisms (the equality of those who are not equal); and b) the natural way of life within the community and, by extension, any social form reproduced "economically," "automatically" and "natu-rally," in which a generalized participation poses no danger to the reproduction of the system. As Kalbfleish has rightly stated,

> democracy entails a permanent contradiction, since when it corresponds to a situation in which the exploitation structure is to a certain point reproduced and extended economically and automatically, it then becomes a formal apparatus. When it corresponds to situations in which the State intervenes polit-ically as a means of reproducing the economy, however, de-mocracy then becomes an obstacle to development.[5]

The automatic reproduction of society (the immanent struc-ture) would mean capitalism in its purest state, which does not exist; although it is true that in the "classic" moments of certain countries (such as the United States, England and France) capitalism has come close to this ideal "purity." Its evolution, however, neces-sarily leads to the development of authoritarian tendencies that in-crease the erosion of what is already a critical "automatism" in civil society. This "automatism" would thus seem to be transferred to the political apparatus in the form of a grotesque simulacrum of techno-cratic democracy.[6] This profound crisis of the State greatly aggra-vates the "middle classes" who—by reading and re-reading the Scriptures and the classics—seek visions of a war (and a symbiosis) between two immense apocalyptic structures, and the prediction of all kinds of catastrophes.

---

5. Rudi Kalbfleish, *Strukturprobleme der modernen Demokraties,* Stammheim: Karp und Sohnen Verlag, 1977.

6. As described by Philip K. Dick in his novel *The Simulacra,* New York: Ace Books, 1964. I should mention in passing—before I forget—that all the authors quoted in this chapter (except Dick) are actually characters in this novel and that the works referred to in this chapter have been invented. The quoted texts are part of a small political theory sim-ulacrum.

XI   The West: The Garden of Democracy

(Strength)

"*But leave out the outer court and do not measure it, because it has been handed over to pagans.*"

Rev. 11:2

The great crisis which Marxism and the Communist Movement have undergone has greatly fertilized and broadened the worker's struggle in favor of new alternatives; this crisis has, moreover, opened the doors to intellectual and political creativity which remained closed for many years due to the stone and mud of Stalinism. The crisis has also provoked many a change and stimulated new attitudes. One of these attitudes is to seek—given the evidence of first-hand experience that times have changed—theoretical nourishment by reading and re-reading the Marxist classics in a search for conceptual instruments that may throw light on the new situation. Thus we are bewildered to discover the amazing wealth and many-sided nature of Marx, Engels and Lenin's thought concealed by Stalinist orthodoxy. Many Marxist trends were born this way, all naturally and creatively seeking to establish their link with the enriching discussions carried out by pre-Stalinist Marxists and by persecuted Marxists from the so-called "personality cult" period. Re-reading the classic Marxists has confirmed, moreover, the inevitable fact that important gaps do exist—particularly regarding political theory—which became particularly evident when an attempt was made to explain the new kinds of capitalist States in imperialist countries (fascism, monopolistic State capitalism), the peculiarities of power structures in countries with a colonial past (dependency, dictatorships), the characteristics of the actual Stalinist phenomenon (dictatorship of the proletariat, lack of political democracy in socialist conditions, repression), and the peculiar transition to liberal democracy and capitalism started in 1989 in Central Europe.

A degree of anxiety and hopelessness concerning the loss of an "original unity and purity" has activated a persistent and ancient defense mechanism. In other words, practical and direct research regarding the new reality is substituted with overwhelming frequency by prolonged immersions in the classic texts (Marx, Engels, Lenin) and the semi-classic ones (Gramsci, Luxemburg, Kautsky, and so on), thereby ensuring that new political alternatives are formulated in the most orthodox *form* possible, which means that new situations and alternatives are explained *as if Marx himself had explained them,* endowed with a mysterious prophetic gift. This vice entails serious consequences as they append a bothersome Talmudic burden to discussions of vital importance. It is, for instance, now possible to "prove" that there are foundations in Marx that enable a theory to be established concerning the democratic and pacific path towards socialism; although it has also become possible to "demonstrate" that only the destruction of the bourgeois State and its substitution by a dictatorship of the proletariat can lead to socialism. I obviously have no intention here of denying the indisputable interest that the study of Marxist classical literature affords regarding this issue.

Another danger which this Talmudic re-reading vice entails is that new political alternatives tend to be defined *by means of exclusion.* There is a tendency to demonstrate from the very outset that the characteristics and conditions explained so adroitly by Marx (or Lenin) have ceased to operate. Rather than explain what remains valid nowadays, a new field is defined by using difference *indicators;* this means that a leap is made to the political consequence level without first going into any depth. This elliptical procedure evades the explanation of new phenomena and substitutes it by comparing interpretations of *previous* situations thereby enabling the new phenomenon to be discerned and delimited.

In a certain sense, the origins of the 1989 collapse of socialism in Europe can be founded in the so-called "Eurocommunist" political alternatives developed during the 70s. It is obvious that the *glasnost* and the *perestroika* are peculiar soviet versions of Eurocommunism. But this Eurocommunist alternative was partly curbed and obscured by the elliptical readings of contemporary reality just mentioned above. As a matter of fact, part of the argument as to the possibility of a pacific and democratic way to socialism was defined by means of exclusion, in an attempt to establish the boundaries of "developed" country conditions as opposed to those that prevailed before they became "developed" or to those that prevail in "under-developed" countries. This argument was linked to the idea that traits which are insufficiently democratic in socialist countries stem from an "underdeveloped" or "barbarous" historical past. A study of the State carried out by French communists shows that the Leninist dictatorship of the proletariat consists of a *power of the "majority" which temporarily lacks a "majority,"* since it is the outcome of a revolution in a "semi-Asiatic" country where a backward non-proletarian (peasant) mass predominated and had to be won over to the revolution *after* the conquest of power. According to these French communists, the 19th century bourgeois State that Marx and Engels were familiar with was essentially repressive and in a sense "semi-feudal."[1] In Western developed and contemporary capitalist countries, on the contrary, the working class constitutes the majority, which is why *it is possible to establish the power of the "majority" with the support from the "majority"* by means of elections and from the outset. Fabre, Hincker and Sève have stated that:

> Both the impossibility of eluding a civil war and the proletarian weakness are a rule in the early stages of mankind's step towards socialism and in countries where capitalism is hardly developed."[2]

These authors add, however, that this "rule" cannot be applied to a period in which socialism on a world scale is more powerful than capitalism, or to countries where the working class is numerous, educated, organized, and can center around the majority of the people and thereby go a step further towards socialism. In brief, the exploited class in "developed" countries is no longer that dehumanized, uncultured, ignorant, fearful and incoherent mass Lenin referred to. It is evident, however, that the fact the majority in any given country are wage-earners (intelligent, cultivated, educated, courageous and coherent!) and that the proletariat is more numerous, is not sufficient to attain an electoral majority as regards a

1. Jean Fabre, François Hincker, Lucien Sève, *Les communistes et l'Etat,* Paris: Editions Sociales, 1977, pp. 21, 23, 55 and 56. In 1936, French society was still mostly peasant (p. 83).
2. *Ibid.,* p. 58.

socialist transformation program. Over half a century ago, Kelsen's polemic vis-à-vis Marxism was stated in the following terms:

> Why is mere political democracy not transformed into another kind of economic democracy—which is to say, why is it that a bourgeois-capitalist group governs instead of a proletarian-communist one if the proletariat, shaped by a socialist mentality, constitutes a majority, and the suffrage of the majority ensures the predominance of the Parliament? . . . .The reason why civil democracy stops at the stage of mere political equality, without the latter leading to economic "equality," is that—as the experience of recent revolutions has demonstrated, particularly the Russian one—the proletariat interested in economic equality and the consequent statism or socialization of production is—contrary to what socialism has asserted for many decades and at least up until now—is far from constituting the great majority of the population and forms only a weak minority.[3]

The problem has not been properly stated here, since the possibility of reaching a *majority* is defined in terms of the numerical accumulation of workers and wage-earners and in terms of the existence of a "higher" technical and educational development. The problem is actually far more complex since this "majority" implies—in addition to the number of votes—a political, cultural and ideological hegemony capable of substituting the former bourgeois hegemony. The requisite for determining the conditions that may favor a transition to socialism is not merely the confirmation of the greater presence of workers in developed countries (which is obvious) but, among other things, the knowledge of the *new forms of bourgeois hegemony*.

An acute critic such as Fernando Claudín has also found himself attracted by the assimilation of a *truly* democratic and socialist path leading to this vague and ill-defined socioeconomic space known as "western developed countries": The *basic* difference between the revolution in the West and revolutions in backward countries lies, in fact, in that the former, as opposed to the latter, is the

---

3. Hans Kelsen, *Vom Wesen und Wert der Demokratie,* Aalen: Scientia Verlag, 1963.

work—without which no revolution can take place—of an objective majority subjectively interested in socialism.[4]

This author tells us that since the proletariat is a minority in backward countries and since a low level prevails among the productive forces, only "intermediate revolutions" can take place—not socialist ones—which lead to phases of State capitalism and other class-based systems "which although are not actually capitalist, cannot be considered socialist either, such as the case of Soviet and similar regimes."[5] Any idea attempting to prove that a pacific and democratic path to socialism is viable in certain countries through *a major "development" of the population and the productive forces* (more workers and skills, better wage-earners and technology) inevitably leads to a blind alley, reducing the possibility of an objective understanding. This idea is as barren as its counterpart—very fashionable a few years ago—which proposes that real socialism can at present only be possible in backward countries dominated by imperialism, since that is where contradictions are particularly acute.

The modern Western State is conceived as that beautiful and ancient European lady who, with a graceful movement of her hegemōnic hands, is able to control class violence. Although this is undoubtedly a beautiful image, it does not correspond to reality. There is no point in wasting time to prove that nothing in the history or structure of the so-called "developed" Western countries indicates the presence of conditions leading to true democratic socialism and their absence in backward countries. We should remember—and thereby avoid making crude and inflexible generaliz-

---

4. F. Claudìn, *Eurocomunismo y socialismo,* Madrid: Siglo XXI, 1977, p. 156.

5. *Ibid.,* pp. 146–47. It is a pity that a book with so many valuable elements should also introduce such banal and Eurocentric ideas regarding underdeveloped countries; after suggesting some strange intermediate revolutions to the third world, Claudìn brings in a sketch of political alliances identical to those put into practice by various socialist countries: "An aboslutely essential condition for the possibility of a European socialist process is the alliance of its protagonists with developing people and States that confront imperialism and need the solidarity of European workers just as the latter need theirs . . . world juncture is pressuring to reach a group elaboration of Eurocommunist and European socialist country parties, together with 'third world' anti-imperialist forces" (see p. 179). This is to say that since there will be no authentic socialism in the Third World for the time being, the role of "underdeveloped" countries is to be a "Third World" and "anti-imperialist" support force, while Europeans show everyone just how the true socialist revolution should be carried out.

ations—that during this century the developed West has produced millions of dead in two world wars as well as many colonial wars, and that it has engendered the most appalling forms of fascist dictatorship.

World classification—for the purposes of political analysis—into West and East, development and underdevelopment, should be approached cautiously since this is an ideological expression which only vaguely reflects—and with a high degree of distortion—the history of colonialism and imperialism. The general confirmation, according to which the importance of the non-proletarian masses diminishes proportionately to capitalist "development," consequently fertilizing the democratic field, is entirely inadequate. It becomes paramount to determine concretely the kind of non-proletarian mass that exists in each "backward" country, and the specific and particular characteristics of the proletarian mass in "developed" countries. It is a highly complex problem, since a considerable portion of what is often considered to be a peasant population in backward countries is in fact an intensely poverty-stricken and proletarianized mass of semi-unemployed agricultural workers; although, on the other hand—as has been argued already—a very important part of the population in "developed" countries is linked to strictly non-capitalist processes (services, State apparatus), which is why it can be classified in a sense as a "non-proletarian mass." In both cases the massive presence of population layers inserted in not strictly capitalist activities tends to produce political effects of great import, closely linked to concrete forms whereby the ruling class achieves a solid hegemony and a high degree of legitimacy.

This takes us to a typically Eurocommunist proposal—in the Gramscian tradition—which refers to the nature of the capitalist State in the developed Western world.[6] According to this proposal, there would be a State expansion and broadening in the West characterized by a potential contradiction between the State's role in organizing the socio-economic configuration and its function as an instrument of the monopolistic bourgeoisie. This contradiction

---

6. Régis Debray, formerly a fiery defendant of the Third World and a Eurocentrist at present, upholds that "if anything new is to occur it will be in the Old Continent or nowhere," *Lettre aux communistes français et à quelques autres,* Paris: Seuil, 1978, p. 15.

would generate a State crisis—not entailing a classic revolutionary crisis—which would enable the monopoly-State relationship to be destroyed and its social and economic functions to be preserved *without an important modification of the State apparatus as a whole.*[7] In previous revolutionary situations (particularly in 1917 Russia), however, it became necessary to *destroy the State,* which is to say, to destroy the institutional materialization of the bourgeoisie-petty bourgeoisie alliance, due to the fact that in such cases—unlike those in the West—the political crisis never goes through the State apparatus.[8]

In brief, this would bring about, in Gramsci's terms, two polarized situations: the *revolution in the East,* characterized by a war of movements and frontal attacks, within the context of a "primitive and gelatinous" civil society; and the *revolution in the West,* predominated by the war of positions and in which the presence of a strong civil society with deeply-rooted democratic traditions must be taken into account. Under such conditions, the State is cross-cut by the class cleavages since we have here, as Santiago Carrillo put it, a mass State apparatus.[9]

These proposals point in the right direction, although two major mistakes can be discerned.

The first is the denial of the concept that the new State forms are a new kind of alliance block. Lenin used to say that the peasant masses—which had, so far, formed the supporting basis of the bourgeois-petty bourgeois block in power—could only be drawn once the proletariat was in power. In the West, however, it is possible— or so they say—to establish a wide antimonopolistic front *before* power is taken. The latter political slogan has blinded many to the State's new characteristics, to the extent that this kind of statement has been made in France:

> The great monopolistic bourgeoisie nowadays dominates with-
> out sharing and maintains the rest of the capitalist social layers
> in a state of dependency, particularly at an economic level. It

---

7. Christine Buci-Glucksmann, "Sur le concept de crise de l'Etat et son histoire," in *La crise de l'Etat,* pp. 59–88.

8. *Ibid.,* pp. 87–88.

9. Santiago Carrillo, *Demain l'Espagne,* (interviews with Régis Debray and Max Gallo), Paris: Seuil, 1976, p. 190.

would be naive to think they form a block *in power,* since the actual power belongs to the monopolies.[10]

The Spanish Communist Party's *Manifesto-Program* claimed that the present State is the "exclusive instrument of monopolistic layers."[11]

It is inaccurate to conceive of the Western modern State as a garden of democracy and socialization dominated by a barren isle of monopolistic capital, or as the outer court open to the populace of a monopoly-occupied temple. What, in fact, appears to be the "State crisis" is, in many cases and as far as I see it, a crisis of transition towards a new model of hegemony and legitimacy—and, consequently, a modification of the block in power—whereby the bourgeoisie attempts to lay down the foundations for a network of alliances that will encompass, in addition to various bourgeois layers, the new "non-proletarian masses." Unlike the so-called premonopolistic State, however, in which non-proletarian masses embodied a civil society atomized and *separated* from the State (with the consequent illusion of the State's autonomy and supremacy), the modern State tends to lose its autonomous form—separated from society—and shapes a new system of legitimizing illusions, namely the social State and despotic society. Such tendencies can be clearly seen nowadays in Germany and the United States. What was outlined in previous chapters regarding marginality thus becomes an approximation to the problem of the modern State's new forms.

The possibilities of a pacific and democratic transition towards socialism must therefore be understood within the framework of this "State crisis," a crisis possibly leading to a turning point in which the socialist revolution is no longer "exclusively necessary to the proletariat, but to the immense majority of the population";[12] although it could also lead to the consolidation of a block of classes headed by the monopolistic capital adopting the antiliberal form of postindustrial "new politics." Nothing is predetermined, and false optimism should be avoided. It thus becomes imperative to under-

10. Fabre, Hincker, Sève, *Les Communistes,* p. 130.
11. Quoted by F. Claudín, *Eurocomunismo,* p. 128. Claudín is right in pointing out that non-monopolistic capital is integrated into a global mechanism, the hegemony of which is in the hands of monopolistic capital.
12. Santiago Carrillo, *Demain,* p. 52.

score that *the very conditions which are supposed to make the formation of a majority in favor of socialism possible, simultaneously constitute a new form of capitalist, postindustrial and, quite probably, I'm afraid, postdemocratic State.*

The second major mistake contained in some Eurocommunist formulations lies in the mechanical separation of the "revolution in the East" from the "revolution in the West." This mistake has two serious consequences. The first is the absolute confusion it introduces concerning the interpretation of the so-called third world, the world of the war of movements and of the gelatinous and primitive civil society. One need only think of countries such as India, Egypt, Algeria or Mexico to realize the existence of an extraordinarily complex State structure, of highly developed legitimizing and mediating forms, of an important expansion of social and monopolistic State activities, and so on, all of which are—in theory—conditions for reaching a "majority in favor of socialism" despite the mass presence of non-proletarian rural population and of the recent (or nonexistent) nature of classic democratic mechanisms. A great heterogeneity of situations exists in the so-called third world, just as the twenty or so "democratic and developed" countries do not form a homogeneous world.

The second consequence, closely linked to the first, is the historicist and deterministic implication which the East/West dichotomy entails. In the same way that Russia, due to its semi-Asiatic and underdeveloped nature, was determined to organize power for a "majority" that was temporarily a "minority" (although "temporarily" became, at best, many years of Stalinism), countries of the modern Gramscian East have no other option but to exert an antidemocratic violence leading to "totalitarian socialism." China, Cuba and Vietnam could be seen as "proofs" of this concept. The fundamental problem of the relationship between democracy and socialism is thereby shifted to the realm of historicist determinism; the fundamental reasons behind the democracy-socialism fusion failure in Eastern countries could be determined by their very origins, by their original condition as backward countries—by a presocialist "original sin" of sorts.[13]

---

13. An example of this conception is provided by Jean Ellenstein's *Histoire du phénomène stalinien,* Paris: Grasset, 1975.

One need only return to "good old Marx" who though of socialism as the product of the most advanced capitalism (19th century capitalism, nevertheless) in order to predict that, this time, the doors of true socialism are being opened in developed Western countries. One would have to read the classics very carefully to discover that actual history has not yet tainted "true socialism." The tragicomic fact about these kinds of journeys to "good old Marxism" is clear when we confront the 1989 collapse of communism in Europe. *Perestroika* and the end of the Berlin Wall proved that what failed was not a strange Oriental socialism, but the very way in which Western civilization created a space for the "dictatorship of proletariat."

XII Capitalism and Democracy

(The Hanged Man)

And the dragon stopped in front of the woman as she was having the child, so that he could eat it as soon as it was born from its mother. The woman brought a male child into the world, the son who was to rule all the nations with an iron scepter.

Rev. 12:4–5

Those who place greater emphasis on modern society's "permanent and structural" processes are inclined to develop economism-oriented ideas concerning the functions of the capitalist State and strongly support the idea that *democracy is the typical form of the capitalist State.*

On the other hand, those who find "historical and occasional" elements to be of great importance tend to support voluntaristic and even spontaneistic ideas on politics. They foster above all the thesis that *democracy is an achievement attained by means of the popular and proletarian struggle against capitalist class interests.*[1]

Neither of these two conclusions is false. The first case considers democracy as the formal and normal outcome of capitalist market economy (as the expression of a central order which must cope with market chaos as well as with a political expression of labor freedom.) The second case considers democracy as the crystallization of a political force relationship.

Having stated this, two major problems still remain unresolved: a) Why has the bourgeois class—an absolute minority within society—managed to reach a stable and apparently permanent consensus in certain countries, whereas the proletariat has not reached a formal (electoral) consensus in capitalist countries and lacks the conditions which would enable its institution in countries where power has been taken over by revolutionary means? b) How can one account for despotic and authoritarian tendencies and the fact that liberal democracy has been, is at present, and seems

---

1. Gramsci was already aware of the dangers of falling into these two interpretations of history: "L'errore in cui si cade spesso nella analisi storica consiste nel non saper trovare il repporto tra il 'permanente' e lo 'ocasionale', cadendo così o nell' esposizione di cause remote come se fossero quelle immediate, o nell' affermazione che la cause immediate sono le sole cause efficienti" (Notebook 4).

destined to be in the near future a *minority* phenomenon within the great international capitalist concert?

If "bourgeois" democracy is considered to be the typical capitalist superstructure with a tendency to emerge with the development of industrialization, an answer to the first question could be glimpsed—although the development of authoritarian and dictatorial forms of government (fascist or not) remains unclear. In the face of this, orthodox and dogmatic statements found in Marxist manuals remain barren as do the theses of Lipset and Rostow.[2] Often enough a nebulous working class or bourgeoisie "authoritarianism" is adopted, or else old liberal and evolutionist ideas.

Yet if, on the contrary, democracy is the result of a political balance between antagonistic classes, it becomes possible to understand that the defeats or weaknesses of the working class are paid for with strong doses of authoritarianism, although in this case the consensus phenomenon acts merely as a balancing point without a reality of its own.

Let us look carefully at the problems posed by these two opposite conceptions. Recent political tendencies on a world scale seem to confirm that there is no logical and natural relationship between the institution of democracy and the development of capitalism. The facts that prove this can be roughly classified into three major tendencies:[3]

I. The increased limitation of concurrence mechanisms; this is to say that the concentration of economic and political power in large monopolies and societies severely restricts the liberal principles of the free market and of egalitarian electoral participation in political decisions. This includes the growing power of the mass media which "models" public opinion according to the interests of great economic corporations.

II. The reinforcement of authoritarian and despotic control tendencies in the actual factory—which is to say in the highly hier-

---

2. Seymour Martin Lipset, *Political Man, the Social Basis of Politics*, Garden City, N.Y.: Doubleday, 1960. W. W. Rostow, *Politics and the Stages of Growth*, Cambridge: Cambridge University Press, 1971.
3. According to Samuel Bowles and Herbert Gintis's excellent summary, "Le poing invisible," *Le monde diplomatique*, July 1978.

archical production and organization processes of the increasingly complex economic systems.

III. The growing social homogenization that creates an immense wage-earning majority. This is to say, the extinction of a large number of non-capitalist groups and social layers that helped to form multiclassist parties structured on conflicts that were not determined by social class division boundaries.

The realization afforded by these considerations is that democratic institutions were not a gift from the bourgeoisie. In fact, the consolidation of liberal democracy is not that old. It is not much older than a century in most developed countries (not even fifty years, strictly speaking; in England, for instance, it was not until 1928 that women were given full voting rights). It is also quite clear that the triumph of civil rights and universal suffrage runs parallel to those concerning salary increases, higher living standard, social welfare benefits and union rights. But it is evident, however, that all these triumphs have not altered the foundations of the development of capitalist exploitation, and that such victories not only did not hamper the actual capitalist structure but, on the contrary, generally found in liberal democracy and additional element with which to oil the complex reproduction apparatus of social relationships within capitalist production. This assertion, however, in no way undermines the argument that representative—or "formal," "bourgeois"—democracy now constitutes more than ever a powerful weapon as regards the working class struggle.

It is crucial to underscore that "formal" democracy has in no way exclusively—and frequently not even fundamentally—lent legitimacy and consensus to the ruling class. We must not suppose, therefore, that the "crisis of democracy" created by the development of capitalism's most modern monopolistic tendencies implies in the least a mechanical correlative weakening of the bourgeoisie in the balance of forces. A close examination of the history of capitalism shows that democracy is not the sole legitimacy-lending mechanism and that *consensus under non-democratic conditions* also exists. A study of these conditions—widespread in the third world—enables the democratic phenomenon to be placed within the larger context of *mediation structures*. The presence within society of boundaries and fractures either of precapitalist origin or with a non-capitalist basis has not only enabled multiclassist parties to be formed, but has also in very many cases been the condition for the development of non-democratic stable forms of political power as well as relatively despotic ones.[4] These are not merely exceptional forms based on repression, but stable regimes such as Egypt's Nasserism, Argentina's Peronism or Mexico's institutional revolutionary regime, to name but a few. On the other hand—and at another level—fascism proved a bitter lesson. These phenomena are in no way archaic, although they prefigure the most dangerous tendencies of the modern State.

In representative democratic systems, as in stable non-democratic forms, a *political decision space* is engendered, to which citizens have access in one way or another, and to which they are called to "decide." This space is constituted by means of a contradiction-displacing process (whether through legal, political, economic, cultural or psychological mechanisms), based on the existence of conflicts which only indirectly express the capital/work contradiction. Citizens are thus called on to make a "decision"—whether through elections, or by corporative means—concerning a group of issues upon which the survival of the dominating exploitation system does not in fact depend.

In an interesting discussion with Italian communist intellectuals, Norberto Bobbio defined the prevailing significance of democracy as "a group of rules (called the rules of the game) which enable the broadest and safest participation of most citizens, whether directly or indirectly, in political decisions, which is to say the decisions that interest the collectivity."[5]

The "rules of the game" organize everyone's free right to vote for real alternatives—using the numerical majority principle—and without diminishing the rights of the minority who continue in the game that will eventually turn them into the majority. The essential problem does not lie in the actual rules of the game; one could argue endlessly as to all the ploys that hinder the effectually equal repre-

4. For further development of this topic, see, Bartra, *El poder despótico burgués*.
5. Norberto Bobbio, "¿Qué alternativas a la democracia representativa?," in *El marxismo y el Estado,* Barcelona: Avance, 1977, p. 49.

sentation of every layer of the population (for instance, indirect voting, non-proportionality, circumscription division), until each is—theoretically—eliminated and a mathematically "perfect" system can be claimed. The fundamental problem lies, however, in the way in which a given society defines the field of *political decisions,* as opposed to the field of elements in terms of which *it is not possible* to take decisions—or has at least not been considered to be socially necessary. The above-described is a process of historical accumulation whereby capitalist society gradually builds the spaces according to what can and cannot be decided—regarding either technical, economic, moral or political matters—even as it organizes the levels and means of decision. For instance, whereas in certain periods and societies the death sentence is a matter that can be decided, in others this problem falls within the area of what cannot be decided either on a short- or long-term basis. There is also another set of "moral" principles which radically block the possibility of voting and deciding as regards certain themes (such as so-called human rights, which are violated, although not in any form legitimized by the "rules of the game"). On the other hand, it is obvious that the decision area has what could be called technical limits due to the fact that only "experts" can understand the problem or else because scientific development has not reached the necessary level for the decision to be made.

What I am particularly interested in pointing out here, though, is the constitution of an essentially economic space, which "functions automatically," and reproduces itself, growing in a "natural" and "autonomous way"—with a variable degree of political intervention—in a similar way to the air we breathe (air which must be "protected," particularly in large cities, but which need not be "made" and which we are not called on to decide whether we should breathe it or not). This air that envelops us in an apparently natural and spontaneous way in capitalist society, becomes the commodity examined by Marx when he began his study of capital production. This relative automatism of capital production has allowed the class struggle to exhale from everyday life, so to speak, ancient forms of extraeconomic coercion; although automatism has stimulated too the development of forms of political control of the economy that have shaped the physiognomy of the modern "social State."

In clamoring for the superiority and preservation of the *citizen's rights* and for their institutionalization (the separation between the citizens' self-government and the mechanisms of so-called social democracy), Bobbio fails to realize that the key to its existence lies in the self-regulation of the "worker's rights"—which is to say, of the economy. Capitalist economy has managed to do this, although it has done so by automatizing exploitation. The challenge faced by socialism is the self-regulation of equality, which will begin the State's journey towards self-extinction.

We could claim that the *condition* for the relative stability of representative democracy institutions and of authoritarian and despotic government forms is the combination of two situations. The first would be the presence of not strictly capitalist elements (whether originated in the *ancien régime* or the outcome of modern capitalist State "socialization" forms) that constitute the main social basis supporting bourgeois parties or Bonapartist-type governments; these elements also generate a socio-political culture capable of delimiting the *political decision zone* without making an attempt on mechanisms of capital production (quite the contrary, in fact). The second would be the existence of self-regulating production system functions which are essentially *economic* and are only under the State's *political* jurisdiction at times of severe crises.

These basic conditions determine capitalist society's real possibility of reaching—with more or less developed democratic ingredients—a political form firmly established in the "consensus" of the governed. These conditions, however, do not determine the capitalist State's concrete form which is historically fashioned by the social struggles in each country and each area. Thus, although representative democracy is not the typical form of capitalist power (there is no such thing as a *typical* form, in fact), capitalist society establishes economic conditions that enable its development—should popular struggles impel it—without the collapse of the system. It is true that the expansion and broadening tendencies of State apparatuses do provoke a major change in the conditions of the system's economic and political reproduction, mainly because they severely restrict or corner the self-regulating functions of capital production. For this very reason, however, it becomes impossible to claim categorically that the State's "social functions" could be used to regulate and plan a socialist society. This is effectually possible, although this possibility is not based exclusively on the existence of a social mass State but chiefly on the presence of a sturdy *worker and popular movement which is radically autonomous and detached from the State.* The expansion, on its own, of the State's social functions can easily provoke authoritarian and antidemocratic tendencies even as it prefigures mechanisms that prove vital to a socialist type of planning.

The so-called Eurocommunist movement helped to understand the extraordinarily "subversive" potential of the struggle for democracy confronted by the capitalist system's increasingly despotic tendencies.[6] It should be said, however, that this alternative can become truly innovative only insofar as the struggles become of an international nature and are not brought to a standstill by East-West borderlines—whether these are regarded as dividing the world into capitalist and socialist countries or as barriers that distinguish development from underdevelopment (sometimes referred to as a North-South polarity.)

In both underdeveloped and socialist countries, people have the same objective need to reach or develop the democracy obtained by the masses in developed capitalist western countries, as an imperative condition for impelling socialism. In fact, it is due to the democratic struggles in underdeveloped countries and socialist nations that the fight for an advanced democracy in the developed Western world itself has become up-dated. These struggles have become symbolized by the great tragic experiences of Chile's Popular Unity and Dubcek's government in Czechoslovakia.[7] It is mostly thanks to peripheral experiences—whether of a capitalist or socialist nature—that the role and importance of world scale democracy has become somewhat more transparent. The imperialist forces that

6. The term "Eurocommunist" should be abandoned, together with its western and Eurocentric implications.
7. We should add, of course, the XX Congress of the Communist Party of the USSR, Vietnam's liberation, China's cultural revolution, the Cuban revolution's and the 1968 popular and student movements. These phenomena restated in one way or another the problems of democracy, hegemony and the State in the contemporary world.

seemed about to engender Western democracy—threatened, supposedly, by the dragon of the popular revolutionary movement—have ended by giving birth to a political system that seeks to "rule all the nations with an iron scepter." It must be admitted, however, that the melting of representative democracy within social democracy has not as yet produced an authentic political alternative.

XIII Stalin-666

(Death)

If anyone is clever enough he may interpret the number of the beast: it is the number of a man, the number 666.

Rev. 13:18

Let us proceed now to another entirely different setting where the simulacrum of a war was spectacularly enacted; a war which—despite the fact it reflected a bloody social and political struggle—was elevated in imaginary spirals to amazing political and judicial heights of fiction. The drama's Demiurge was Stalin, who conceived a series of shows—the three great Moscow trials— which enacted, with all the contrivances of a new demonology, the tragedy of a revolution that devoured itself.

As in any other religion, Stalinism staged—in what could be regarded as three allegorical plays—a dualist conception of the sacred and the profane. The three great Moscow trials were one of the principal mechanisms whereby the definition of what was *pure, sacred, patriotic* and *socialist* was established to counteract *treason, deviations* and *profane activities*. In these great trials the most bloodly and atavistic aspect of the new ideology surfaced, justifying the persecution and repression of a large mass of leaders, militants, intellectuals and laymen.

The following is a transcription—by way of a play-like *collage*—of some scenes in this simulacrum; its aim is to introduce and stimulate meditation about the problems that arise vis-à-vis the transition towards socialism.

SCENE I
(Introduction)

The curtain rises slowly: Moscow, winter 1938. In the left-hand corner of the stage, seated in the dock, is Bukharin, one of the great leaders and theorists of the Bolshevik Party. He is making his final statement.

BUKHARIN. World history is a universal court . . . the whole country is behind Stalin. He is the hope of the world, he is the creator.[1]

At the other end of the stage a spotlight suddenly lights up the court usher, who acts here as narrator and secret devil's advocate; his whispering voice, magnified by the microphones, is heard to say:

USHER: Marxism has not only been transformed into the official religion; it also celebrates grand vindicating ceremonies against the "enemies" of the socialist motherland.

From his dais the sadly celebrated USSR prosecutor Vyshinsky is concluding his requisition against Bukharin, Rikov, Yagoda, Krestinski, Rakovski and sixteen others accused of espionage, murder and treason with the following invocation:

VYSHINSKY: Our whole country, the young and the old, await and clamor for one thing only: that the traitors and spies who sold our country to the enemy be shot like mangy dogs!

Our people demand only one thing: that the damned reptiles be crushed!

Time will pass. Weeds and thistles will infest the graves of the execrated traitors, of those who are the object of the eternal contempt of honest soviet men, of all the soviet people.

And above our heads, above our happy country, our clear and radiant sun will continue to shine with its luminous rays. Along a path from which the last stain and the last vileness of the past has been removed, we all, our people, guided by our well-beloved leader and master, the great Stalin, shall continue to march forward, always forward, towards communism!

USHER: How was it possible to justify this historical and irrational aggression towards the most brilliant and outstanding leaders of the October Revolution? How did the accused themselves and the majority of the people agree to the Stalinist trials and to confess to the worst crimes?

Curtain

---

1. All quotes have been taken from *Le procès du "Bloc des droitiers et des trotskistes" antisoviétique devant le Collège Militaire de la Cour Suprême de l'URSS contre: Boukharine, A. I., Rykov, G. C., Yagoda, N. N., Krestinski, Ch. G., Rakovski* (and 16 other accused) *Compte rendu sténographique des débats (du 2 au 13 mars 1938), publié par le Commissariat du Peuple de la Justice de L'URSS*, Moscow, 1938, 850 pp.

SCENE II

(The Incident)

USHER: As everyone knows, the whole trial was based on the confessions of the guilty parties. After the indictment was read—in which they were defined as traitors, spies, inciters and murderers—the accused admitted their crimes in the form of a litany.

THE PRESIDENT: Accused Bukharin, do you plead guilty of the deeds of which you are accused?

BUKHARIN: Yes, I plead guilty of the deeds of which I am accused.

THE PRESIDENT: Accused Rikov, do you plead guilty of the deeds of which you are accused?

RIKOV: Yes, I plead guilty.

THE PRESIDENT: Accused Yagoda, do you plead guilty of the deeds of which you are accused?

YAGODA: Yes, I plead guilty.

USHER: But, unexpectedly—or apparently, at any rate—one of the accused decides not to plead guilty, an event which evolves into a revealing situation of what previous cross-examinations must have been like.

THE PRESIDENT: Accused Krestinski, do you plead guilty of the deeds of which you are accused?

KRESTINSKI: I plead not guilty. I am not a Trotskyist. I have never formed part of the "block of right-wing Trotskyists," whose existence I ignored. I have not committed a single crime which is imputed to me personally; I particularly plead not guilty of maintaining relationships with the German espionage service.

USHER: After some confusion, during which the president reminded the accused of his confession in previous proceedings to the crimes now denied, the ceremonial continued with the rest of the accused continued.

CHORUS OF ACCUSED: Yes, I plead guilty. Yes, I plead guilty. Yes, I plead guilty. Yes, I plead guilty. Yes, I plead guilty. Yes, I plead guilty. Yes . . .

USHER: During the following cross-examinations, prosecutor

Vyshinsky vented his cruelty on Krestinski, harassing him continually. The logic behind the cross-examination did not lie in the search for proofs but in the confession obtained, in an evil exertion of a vicious dialectic.

VYSHINSKY: You have declared you were in a special conspiratorial situation. What do you mean by a "special conspiratorial situation"?

KRESTINSKY: You know very well that. . . .

VYSHINSKY: You will be kind enough not to quote me as a witness in this affair. I am asking you what a "special conspiratorial situation" means.

KRESTINSKI: I have said that in my statement.

VYSHINSKY: You will not answer my questions?

KRESTINSKI: That sentence in which I declare to be in a special conspiratorial situation is written in the statement I made on June 5th or 9th, which is false from beginning to end.

VYSHINSKY: That is not what I am asking you, and I request you not to hasten your answers. I am asking you what "I am in a special conspiratorial situation" means.

KRESTINSKI: It does not correspond to reality.

VYSHINSKY: We shall see that later. What I want to do is discern the meaning of your statement when you said that you were in a "special conspiratorial situation."

KRESTINSKI: If this were to coincide with reality, it would mean that as a Trotskyist I am taking every possible precaution to conceal the fact I am Trotskyist.

VYSHINSKY: Perfect. And in order to conceal this you must deny your Trotskyism?

KRESTINSKI: Yes.

VYSHINSKY: You now declare you are not a Trotskyist. But are you not doing this to conceal the fact you are a Trotskyist?

KRESTINSKI: (after a silence). No, I declare I am not a Troskyist.

VYSHINSKY: (addressing the Court) May I cross-examine accused Rosengolz? Accused Rosengolz, have you listened to this dialogue?

ROSENGOLZ: Yes.

VYSHINSKY: In your opinion, is Krestinski a Trotskyist?

ROSENGOLZ: He is a Trotskyist.

VYSHINSKY: Accused Krestinski, I ask you to listen, or else you will say you have not understood.

KRESTINSKI: I feel ill.

VYSHINSKY: If the accused says he feels ill, I have no right to continue cross-examining him.

Curtain

SCENE III

(Dialectics Continue, or Illegal Legality)

USHER: The next day (and we can imagine Krestinski did not sleep too well that night) the accused recanted, returning to his confessional track.

KRESTINSKI: Yesterday, swayed by a fleeting and acute sense of false shame, due to this atmosphere and to the fact that I was sitting in the dock, as well as to the distressing impression caused by the reading of the indictment and all this aggravated by my illness, I did not state the truth, which is to say, that I plead guilty. Instead of saying, "yes, I plead guilty," I almost mechanically answered, "no, I plead not guilty."

USHER: This would seem as if the famous law by means of which negation is negated had been applied in tragic-comic terms. The first statement ("I plead guilty") was denied; although this denial was in turn immediately denied, ("it is a lie that I plead not guilty.") The "dialectical" logic of the cross-examinations gradually led, in fact, to the creation of a theory about the duality or duplicity of the accused and of life itself. The dialectic was substituted by the judicial procedures and cross-examinations, the evidence replaced by confessions; only the latter could reveal treason and impurity in the behavior of the accused, which was legal and socialist to all appearances. History was, in fact, transformed, as Bukharin said, into a court. . . . Its understanding and transformation were transposed to judicial practices and police procedures.

VYSHINSKY: Tell me frankly, did you use your position as president of the *Centrosoyuz,* an apparatus which had a foreign office, to carry out external counterrevolutionary and antisoviet activities?

ZELENSKY: I think the propagation of tendentious news. . . .

VYSHINSKY: Of tendentious news inciting an antisoviet tendency. Was it an antisoviet activity?

ZELENSKY: The entire bulletin went through meticulous censorship.

THE PRESIDENT: We are not concerned here with official reports.

ZELENSKY: There was nothing else.

VYSHINSKY: Were they tendentious?

ZELENSKY: Yes.

VYSHINSKY: Although they passed censorship?

ZELENSKY: Yes.

VYSHINSKY: You knew how to use legal means to achieve illegal ends?

ZELENSKY: (is silent)

Curtain

SCENE IV

(New Incidents Concerning Dialectics)

USHER: According to Stalinist logic, criminal facts were not proved by confronting them with reality, but by means of a confession in which a counterrevolutionary reality stalked under a revolutionary guise. Bukharin at times took the opportunity to poke fun at Vyshinsky's "dialectics."

VYSHINSKY: Accused Bukharin, is it true or not that a group of your accomplices in the Northern Caucasus held relations with the foreign media of white emigrated cossacks? Is it a fact, yes or no? Rikov has talked about this and so has Slepkov.

BUKHARIN: If Rikov says so, I have no reason not to believe him.

VYSHINSKY: Can't you answer without any philosophy?

BUKHARIN: It is not philosophy.

VYSHINSKY: Without philosophical witticisms?

BUKHARIN: Did I not state that I had explanations concerning this issue?

VYSHINSKY: Say "no."

BUKHARIN: I cannot say "no" and I cannot say that it happened.

VYSHINSKY: So, neither "yes" or "no"?

BUKHARIN: Not at all. Since there are facts that exist although this does not mean they enter the consciousness of a man. It is the problem of the reality of the external world. I am no solipsist.

VYSHINSKY: So, independently from the problem of knowing whether this fact entered or not into your consciousness, did you know about this fact as a conspirator and leader?

BUKHARIN: I did not.

VYSHINSKY: No?

BUKHARIN: But I can answer your question by saying that since that figured in the general plan, I believe it is probable, and given that Rikov talks about it in the affirmative, I have no reason to deny it.

VYSHINSKY: Is it consequently a fact?

BUKHARIN: From the viewpoint of mathematical probability, it could be said with great probability that it is a fact.

VYSHINSKY: You simply do not know how to answer.

BUKHARIN: It is not a matter of "you do not know," but that there are questions which cannot be answered roundly with a "yes" or a "no." It is elemental logic, you know that perfectly well.

VYSHINSKY: Allow me yet to cross-examine Rikov. Did Bukharin know or not about this fact?

RIKOV: I reckon personally, with mathematical probability, that he should have known.

USHER: And so the discussion continued along the same lines. Further on, Vyshinsky ventured to make more deductions.

RIKOV: Bukharin was informed of the existence of the relationship, and knew about it.

VYSHINSKY: That is what I wanted to establish. Allow me to regard it as an established fact that Rikov and Bukharin were informed of the treacherous relationships that also entailed espionage. Rikov, is this exact?

RIKOV: From which espionage derived.

BUKHARIN: So, it turns out that I did know something from which something derived.

VYSHINSKY: You can discuss that when you have some free time.

RIKOV: I'm afraid he won't have that free time.

USHER: The cross-examination continued along these lines. Bukharin ended by exasperating prosecutor Vyshinsky.

VYSHINSKY: It is of little importance whether or not this was the first, do not confirm this encounter took place?

BUKHARIN: Not that one but another equally clandestine.

VYSHINSKY: I am not asking you about your encounters in general, but about this encounter.

BUKHARIN: In Hegel's *Logic* the term "this" is considered as the most difficult. . . .

VYSHINSKY: I request the Court to explain to the accused that he is not a philosopher here but a criminal, and that it is in his interest to abstain from talking about Hegelian philosophy. This would be better, above all for the sake of Hegelian philosophy. . . .

BUKHARIN: A philosopher can well be a criminal too.

VYSHINSKY: Yes, that is to say those who imagine themselves to be philosophers and who are in fact no more than spies. Philosophy has nothing to do here. I am concerned about this encounter, which Jodjaev mentions here. Do you confirm it or deny it?

BUKHARIN: I do not understand the word "this." We had an interview in the country house.

Curtain

SCENE V
(The Final Victory of Dialectics)

USHER: The fact that criticism and self-criticism were exercised under the guise of an accusation and a confession led inevitably to the problem of the duality of characters: criminal-philosopher, revolutionary-antisoviet, legality-illegality. Vyshinsky's very questions pressured all the accused into developing a theory regarding this problem of duality. The trial's dramatic atmosphere focused on the confrontation of confessions which did not fully correspond to others.

BUKHARIN: Yes, he is not telling the truth either. I'm telling you what I knew; as to what they know, that is a matter concerning their own conscience.

VYSHINSKY: Nevertheless, you must explain the fact that three of your old accomplices have testified against you.

BUKHARIN: Look, I do not have enough material and psychological facts for the elucidation of this problem.

VYSHINSKY: You cannot explain it?

BUKHARIN: It is not that I cannot, but that I simply refuse to explain it.

USHER: Towards the end of the trial, however, all the accused attempted to provide an explanation to this phenomenon.

ZELENSKY: Thanks to duplicity and camouflage, I am guilty of having slid into posts reserved for those particularly deserving the party's confidence.

KRAMOV: If I were to say that I was able to defend myself and that I have not wanted to do so, it would be a posture, hypocritical; it would still be that phariseeism, that duplicity which was my disease up until the moment I was arrested.

YAGODA: I became a two-faced man. The *dédoublement* (personality split) began. . . . There were two men. There was one Yagoda, member of the Party who maintained everyday relationships with the rest of the great men of our time; and another Yagoda, motherland traitor and conspirator.

USHER: It was Bukharin, however, who went further in developing the explanation.

BUKHARIN: It thereby seems likely that each of us seated in the dock underwent a singular *dédoublement* of consciousness, an incomplete faith in our counterrevolutionary task. I won't say that this consciousness was missing, but that it was incomplete. This was what brought about this kind of semi-paralysis of the will, this dulling of the reflexes. I think that we are people whose reflexes are curbed to a certain point. This was not due to the absence of consequent ideas, but to the objective

grandeur of the socialist edification. The contradiction between the speed of our degeneration and this dulling of the
reflexes translated the counterrevolutionary situation or that of
the counterrevolutionary who grows within the framework of
the socialist edification in progress. A double psychology was
created here. . . . What emerged was what is called in Hegel's
philosophy a wretched consciousness. This wretched consciousness differed from the ordinary consciousness in that it
was at the same time a criminal consciousness.

Curtain

SCENE VI
(Denouement and Speech)

THE PRESIDENT: . . . Considering the facts above-expounded
and by virtue of articles 319 and 320 of the RSFSR Code of
Criminal Procedure.

> *The Military College of the Supreme Court of the USSR
> sentences:*
> 1. BUKHARIN, Nicolai Ivanovich,
> 2. RIKOV, Alexei Ivanovich,
> 3. YAGODA, Guenrich Grigorevich,
> 4. KRESTINSKY, Nicolai Nicolaievich,
> 5. ROSENGOLZ, Arcadi Pavlovich,
> 6. IVANOV, Vladimir Ivanovich,
> 7. CHERNOV, Mijail Alexandrovich,
> 8. GRINKO, Grigori Fedorovich,
> 9. ZELENSKY, Isaac Abramovich,
> 10. IKRAMOV, Akmal,
> 11. JODJAEV, Faizulla,
> 12. CHARANGOVICH, Vasilii Fomich,
> 13. ZUBAREV, Prokopi Timofievich,
> 14. BULANOV, Pavel Petrovich,
> 15. LEVIN, Lev Grigorievich,
> 16. KAZAKOV, Ignaci Nicolaievich,

17. MAXIMOV-DIKOVSKI, Vaniamin Adamovich (Abramovich) and

18. KRIUCHKOV, Piotr Petrovich,
   to the maximum penalty,

TO BE EXECUTED BY SHOOTING, and to have all their belongings confiscated.

USHER: Ladies and gentlemen, you have just witnessed a spectacular trial in which social and political contradictions were transposed to an imaginary world peopled by "mangy dogs," "traitors," "spies" and "murderers" who faced the honest, courageous and hard-working soviet people. The actors in this judicial drama found themselves inserted in the tumultous and revolutionary crossroads of two symbolic processes; namely, that of the *embourgeoisement* of the proletariat and the proletarianization of the bourgeoisie. Or, to be more precise, the extinction of the bourgeoisie and the bureaucratization of a part of the proletariat. This generated the illusion of *dédoublement* or duplicity which made victims of the accused.

Stalinism unleashed this *dédoublement* as an apparently logical continuation of the general laws of dialectical materialism. The secret to this trial can be looked up in many Stalinist philosophy manuals, in which the classic theses concerning the contradictions, the struggle of opposites, the negation of negation appear all leading to a singluar theory of criticism and self-criticism. This theory was nothing else but the illustration of *repression based on confession*—confession obtained through repression, coercion obtained through repentance. The prosecutor or the policeman held the "criticism" in their hands; the accused had to undergo "self-criticism" so that criticism could prosper.

Zhdanov, a sinister Stalinist theorist, in his celebrated "Speech at the Conference of Philosophy Workers" (1947) formulated the "new theory" in the following terms:

"In our soviet society, where antagonistic classes have been eliminated, the struggle between the old and the new, and, consequently, the development from the inferior to the superior, does not emerge as a struggle between antagonistic classes or as cataclysms—as occurs under capitalism—but as a criticism and self-criticism, that constitutes the true motor force of our development and is a powerful instrument in the hands of the Party. This is, undoubtedly, a new kind of development, a new dialectical law."[2]

This "new law" was undoubtedly a powerful instrument in the hands of the Party which had risen to the category of State, and was manifested in everyday life as the law of repression and self-repression. The confessions and recantations were very important because they were destined to prove the operative power of this dialectic—which is to say that repression came hand in hand with self-repression, just as criticism was inseparable from self-criticism. The reasoning that upheld criticism was based on the existence of self-criticism, whereas self-criticism was unleashed by the severity of repression which, in turn, produced the typical mechanisms of self-repression that led the accused to plead guilty.

Final Curtain

2. Quoted in *Materialism and the Dialectical Method,* London: Lawrence & Wishart, 1952. This small book is a typical example of the Stalinist manual.

XIV Socialist Accumulation and Repression

(Temperance)

Then I saw another angel, flying high overhead, sent to announce the Good News of eternity to all who live on the earth, every nation, race, language and tribe.

Rev. 14:6

It is simply not enough to merely corroborate and denounce the terrible waves of repression during the Stalin period if one seeks to understand the character of the socialist regime in the Soviet Union during the "personality cult" years and after. The hidden springs of Stalinism must be sought in the closely-knit sociopolitical fabric enveloping and tightening around the State and the Party. It has been stated quite rightly that the peculiarities of socialist societies have proved to be a reality impervious to the traditional conceptual instruments of Marxism. It is evident that concepts explaining "necessary correspondence" processes between the "economic basis" and the "superstructure" have as yet only helped to justify Stalinist repression or to skirt the problem by claiming that such phenomena are inscribed within a non-socialist logic. Should the socialist character of the "basis" be admitted, the processes of political repression must be regarded as the defense mechanisms arising from worker and popular victories once they are confronted with an "external enemy" (external to socialism). If, on the contrary, it is acknowledged (as something quite evident) that Stalinist repression is directed towards the demolition of the actual revolutionary political edifice, it becomes difficult to sustain that its determining "basis" was socialist by nature.

Interpretations such as these—prompted by a wish to maintain intact the coherence of the orthodox theoretical model when confronted with the sudden attack of events—leads nowhere. In fact, the oldest Marxist explanations regarding the problem of the dictatorship of the proletariat reveal the need to state anew the economy-polity relationship. The experience of the first worker's government in the world, the Paris Commune, inspired in Engels the following reflection:

> From the very outset the Commune was compelled to recognize that the working class, once come to power, could not go

on managing with the old state machine; that in order not to
lose again its only just conquered supremacy, this working
class must, on the one hand, do away with all the old repressive machinery previously used against itself, and, on the
other, *safeguard itself against its own deputies and officials,* by
declaring them all, without exception, subject to recall at any
moment.[1]

Engels is describing here a new, transitional, situation in
which the working class regards the State as "an evil inherited by the
proletariat" whose "worst sides the victorious proletariat" cannot
avoid cutting off until "a generation reared in new, free social conditions is able to throw the entire lumber of the state on the scrap
heap."[2]

This Marxist concern regarding the danger of the State's survival under socialist conditions was added to another about the possibility that the "transition" State, instead of becoming extinct,
would be strengthened. In the discussions Plekhanov held with pop-
ulists, he repeatedly pointed out the problem; Plekhanov believed
that if the people take power when social conditions are immature,
"the revolution runs the risk of engendering a political monster such
as the ancient Chinese empire or that of the Incas, or in other words,
a renewed czarist despotism, a despotism on a communist foundation.[3]
These ideas have led to a discussion concerning the *premature* nature
of the Russian revolution (and all socialist revolutions in general
which have taken place in the imperialist chain's "weak links.") As
Lucio Colleti has pointed out, the problem of the revolution's "immaturity" is

the problem of building up socialism in a country where there
was still an *accumulation* to be made, an accumulation carried
out in Europe by capitalism and the Industrial Revolution.[4]

1. F. Engels, "Introduction to the Civil War in France," in *Karl Marx: Selected Works,* vol.
II, Moscow: Progress Publishers, 1969, p. 187.

2. *Ibid.,* p. 189.

3. Quoted by Roy Medvedev, *Le stalinisme,* Paris: Seuil, 1972, p. 408. This kind of
interpretation has deteriorated in a crude attempt to apply concepts such as "Oriental despotism" and "Asiatic mode of production" to socialist countries. See R. Bartra, *El modo de
producción asiático,* Mexico: Ediciones Era, 1969.

4. Lucio Coletti, *La cuestión de Stalin,* Barcelona: Anagrama, 1977, p. 39.

The "immaturity" of the socialist process was manifested by means of the double and terrible confirmation that it was being produced "in a single country" that must undergo the pains of a "primitive socialist accumulation."

Although this is evident it can hardly conceal the vagueness of the explanation. If the socialist revolution was *premature,* what determined it? Was it the outbreak of a bourgeois revolution guided by the proletariat towards socialism, as Lenin pointed out once? In this case, though, the notion of the immaturity of the socialist process places the weight of a historical course interpretation on the *moral* decisions of revolutionary party leaders, on those who oriented the revolution towards socialism convinced of the socialist system's intrinsic superiority without considering the historical implications of a political leap that lacked previous economic accumulation.

The fact this *economic accumulation*—implying a greater surplus which has to be channelled into heavy industry sectors and a consequent increase in discipline regarding worker-labor—was necessary to end a state of backwardness, led to the following dilemma, expressed in 1919 by Lukács in dramatic terms:

> Either the individuals constituting the proletariat must realize they cannot help each other unless they proceed to a voluntary reinforcement of work discipline, thereby increasing production; or else, if they are not capable, they must create institutions that are capable of leading to such a state of affairs. In the latter case, they create a legal system through which the proletariat compels its own individual members, the proletarians, to act in accordance with the interests of their class; the proletariat thus turns dictatorship against itself.[5]

Stalinist reality revealed, however, that the dictatorship of the proletariat against itself went far beyond the economic frameworks of an iron-like and disciplined production organization. Clearly, this was partly due to historical reasons—both junctural and hereditary—such as the civil war, imperialist aggression, the world war, economic backwardness, the fact the population was mostly peasant,

---

5. Quoted by Istvan Mészáros, "La question du pouvoir politique et la théorie marxiste," in Il Manifesto, *Pouvoir et opposition dans les sociétés post-révolutionnaires,* Paris: Seuil, 1978, p. 127.

Stalin's personality, and the centralist and bureaucratic traditions of czarism. Jean Ellenstein's analysis of these historical conditions is very interesting; although his conclusion remains incomplete since he has—in his attempt to dissociate the Stalinist phenomenon from socialism—limited his explanation to the circumstantial and specific presence of "deviations" or "excrescences" within the socialist rationality.[6] The problem lies in the fact that socialism cannot be seen nowadays—and far less so in Stalin's day—as a unitary, rounded, closed and immanent system. Socialism is a *transition stage* full of contradictions. It is therefore difficult to establish under such conditions the exact differences between socialism's "deviations" and its nucleus, since the latter is a real tangle of contradictions.

The revolutionary party, nucleus and vanguard of socialist construction, was greatly affected by Stalinist repression. During the '30s, in fact, an extraordinarily accelerated purging of Bolshevik militancy took place. This phenomenon acquired astonishing statistical proportions; the active party members were reduced considerably. At the time of the XVII Congress (1934) there were 2,809,000 members (900,000 of whom were substitutes). During 1935 and 1936 admissions were suspended. The party began again to recruit in November, 1936; from then until the XVIII Congress in 1939, over a million substitute members joined. If natural mortality and withdrawals are taken into account, there should have been 3,500,000 militants (2,600,000 regulars) in 1939; although the census taken at the congress showed only 2,478,000 members (1,590,000 of whom were regulars). Medvedev, who was responsible for these calculations, stated that "only a systematic purging can explain this enormous deficit."[7]

The government apparatus too was subjected to intense purges. It is important to underline that in this case repression tended to affect the pinnacle rather than the militant basis of the apparatus.[8] The same phenomenon was observed in the repression of party militants by means of the following facts: whereas 80 percent of militants had entered the party before 1920, according to 1934

6. Ellenstein, *Histoire du phénomène stalinien.*
7. Medvedev, Le stalinisme, p. 283.
8. *Ibid.,* p. 166.

statistics, only 19 percent of old militants remained five years later.[9] This is to say that practically all the old revolutionary guard—from the topmost leaders to the medium cadre and a substantial part of the militant basis—was eliminated.

Repression at the very heart of the vanguard nucleus had to be explained. This explanation consisted of a curious theory regarding the "duality" of the apparatus. Molotov seems to have been the first to develop, in 1937, the theory according to which the "enemy of the people" could actively participate in the construction of socialism, could support all the party's decisions—without in the least revealing its true enemy nature—so that it could escalate the peak of the bureaucratic apparatus and thus strike the socialist regime all the harder. In the 1937 February-March General Assembly, Molotov announced the following:

> Nowadays the particular danger represented by sabotage and diversion organizations lies in the fact that these saboteurs, these diversion agents and these spies pass for communists and ardent defendants of the soviet regime.[10]

The repression's most dramatic aspect was the fact, impossible to conceal, that it received strong popular support; Medvedev wrote that, "similarly to the Stajanovist movement, the campaign against the "enemies of the people" and the "saboteurs" took on a "mass character."[11] Collective paranoia was unleashed; the belief was spread that an omnipresent clandestine antisoviet organization existed. The starting point was the concept that *given the perfection of socialism, any error must derive from treason.* In January 1937, for instance, the *Sovietskaya Sibir'* newspaper published a revealing statement by the first secretary of Western Siberia's *oblast* Committee, made during a meeting in Novosibirsk:

> We are now so well equipped and have such a devoted personnel that there can be no errors. In the case of an accident or failure in the factory, the first thing to do is seek out the enemy.[12]

9. *Ibid.,* p. 283.
10. *Ibid.,* p. 396.
11. *Ibid.,* p. 400.
12. *Ibid.,* p. 401.

It is important to point out, nevertheless, that this colossal repression of the omnipresent "enemy" also operated as the expression of a complex network of social and economic processes. The general context was that of an intensified class confrontation; the enemies actually existed, although neither in the way nor proportions that were claimed. Repression was inscribed in two great historical junctures of the socialist accumulation process: a) during the 1929–1933 period, repressive violence was closely linked to the accelerated collectivization of agriculture and to the "fight against the kulaks"; b) the second wave of repression (1935–1939) corresponds to a period of political struggle which managed to purge both party and government, and to consolidate Stalinist power through the eradication of every opposition trend. A study of these two periods enables one to understand Stalinist repression as part of basic social and economic processes. It was not a "superstructural" or "relatively autonomous" phenomenon; repression was a peculiar expression of social cleavages in a transitional stage.

The revolutionary process led the USSR towards a socialist construction by strengthening the State apparatus, although the conditions imposing a "primitive socialist accumulation" also engendered a civil society-State fusion by means of the *putrefaction of political power*. What has been ill-termed as Stalin's "mistakes"[13] actually constitute the embodiment of economic accumulation processes which capitalism had not managed to complete in Russia; in this sense, the monstrous expansion of the Stalinist State was the *expression of capitalist elements under socialist conditions*. Capitalist elements crystallized in the accelerated economic growth, which the State channeled and monopolized. And it was precisely the existence of a civil society—in which an admixture of rural backwardness and socialist maturity predominated—which allowed and eased the rapid expansion of the State apparatus. The paradox lay in that the actual *social conditions* which gave impetus to the socialist revolution and which set down the objective bases for the growth of new production relationships were the same ones that enabled the State's expansion. Insofar as the new soviet State appeared to be the carrier

---

13. Bettelheim calls them "inevitable mistakes." *Class Struggles in the USSR. First Period: 1917-1923*, New York: Monthly Review Press, 1976.

of the new life-styles, the society—mature enough for change—offered practically no obstacle to the growing political dictatorship. Under such conditions, whereby the State was expanding precisely thanks to the socialist conditions in which it was immersed, it is hardly surprising Molotov should perceive "enemies" all over the place. The second wave of repression (1935–1939) "solved" this problem by unifying the new national State into a strict ideological monolithism.

Thus Stalinist repression is framed by a double process which the 1917 Revolution accelerated violently: the consummation of the industrial revolution and the consolidation of the unification of the national State. This was produced, however, within the socialist context and fertilized by the October Revolution, which led, in its turn, to another paradox: namely, that State monopoly paralyzed the development of democracy even as it gave impetus to forms of exploitation that did not reproduce themselves in proportion to their intensification. What I mean is that the economic structure ceased to develop according to its own laws, relatively autonomous from political control (which is what occurs with capitalist economy). Economy was developing, on the contrary, under the determination of political processes, under the dictate of the party and the State.

The outcome was an "inversion" of processes: economy was democratized by means of its socialization, whereas politics acquired the despotic rigidity of the economic plans; economy lost the narrow automatism characterizing capitalism, whereas the State assumed functions which turned it into a rigid economic life organizer. The State became the angel of temperance, universal dosage distributor of economic life, magical decanting alchemist daily transforming the good wine of the socialist revolution into stagnant water with which to quench the people's thirst and drown their hopes.

XV Economy and Politics in Socialism

(The Devil)

Seven angels were bringing the seven plagues that are the last of all.

Rev. 15:1

Actual socialism—as we know it nowadays—opens up a space for theoretical reflections that entail revolutionary implications for traditional political concepts. The latter assertion—that might well seem to be evidence—has not, in fact, been seriously taken into account. Most Marxist scholars and non-Marxists have set obstacles in their own path by reaching the conclusion—for a variety of reasons—that contemporary socialist societies should and can be studied *in the same way* as the capitalist system. The path I have chosen is the one followed by such excellent direct studies as those of Rudolf Bahro and Roy Medvedev, analysts who have not been taken in by the attractive though simplistic mirage of establishing similarities between socialist societies and development models of capitalist countries. For instance, the assertion that known forms of socialism are a sort of "State capitalism" is the kind of statement that introduces a confusion of terms, ultimately concealing the new production and reproduction mechanisms of society. This confusion inevitably leads to the analysis of texts and discourses generated by the socialist State itself, thus substituting the study of real processes.[1] "State capitalism" is, at least in its classical Leninist definition, a situation in which the State intervenes in the *regulation* of *private* enterprises; no reference whatsoever is made to a situation in which the State appears as the great "collective capitalist" that practically *excludes* all private enterprises and *subdues* all non-State (cooperative) enterprises. There is a substantial difference between both situations.

The old criticism aimed at socialism by L. von Mises and F. A. von Hayek has, however, triggered a far more enriching polemic.[2] Both economists have sustained the impossibility of making rational

1. This is Bettelheim's case, *Class Struggles*.
2. F. A. von Hayek, editor, *Collectivist Economic Planning*, London, 1935.

calculations regarding production costs under socialist conditions, since collective or State property abolishes the operative function of the market where the monetary value of commodities is automatically determined. "Rationality" should be understood in this process as an automatic process whereby a free competitive market obtains a "balance" in which social mechanisms substitute highly complex calculations that determine "optimum" prices.

Since socialism is a planned mercantile economy in which categories of value, price, salary, profit and rent continue to operate, the relevance of the problems pointed out by Mises and Hayek becomes evident. Indeed, a planning method requires a coherent system that assigns values or prices to commodities in circulation between State and non-State enterprises and in circulation within the State sphere, on one hand, and commodities offered to individual consumers, on the other. Many Marxist economists have set out—in terms of Marxist theory and praxis—to implement a regulating system which may, under socialist conditions, be equivalent to that of the capitalist market. The main problem lies in providing socialism with a self-regulating accumulation process. Many years ago, Dickinson proposed "a kind of simulacrum of a capitalist economy" for socialism, by means of which every process of exploitation pertaining to capitalism would be eliminated, although which, "like capitalism, it would also be moved by the blind election of millions of uncoordinated consumers and producers."[3] Since then, the search for these self-regulating mechanisms has led from Oskar Lange's accountable prices to the *otsenki* ("shadow prices") inscribed in the lineal programming proposed by Kantorovich, and is intensified whenever any plan emerges for developing self-management tending towards decentralization. Paul Sweezy has criticized Lange for wanting to transform planning into a "system of pricing and costing."[4] It is obvious, however, that any decentralization within socialism immediately raises the question of *price politics* regarding commodities which circulates more or less freely within the economy.

3. *Economics of Socialism,* Oxford University Press, 1939, p. 220.
4. *Socialism,* New York, 1949, p. 233, quoted by M. Dobb, *Welfare Economics and the Economics of Socialism: Towards a Commonsense Critique,* London: Cambridge University Press, 1970, p. 188.

All these problems emerged yet again during the soviet "economic reform" in the 60s whereby an attempt was made to establish profitability norms that, according to Evsey Liberman's famous theses, could act as the automatic regulator of the socialist economy, and could be combined with a coherently centralized planning. The purpose of this reform was to increase enterprise independence and reach total financial self-management in all production branches and at all levels.[5] The problem that arises here is that the definition of profitability norms (and, consequently, profit rates) inevitably requires a unity of value (or its equivalent), in addition to a series of regulations concerning the deviation between this unity and prices, not merely so that differential rates may be amended, but so that preferential objectives involved in the accumulation process may be translated into terms of profit and savings rate. This failure of the economic reform seems to indicate Maurice Dobb is right in supporting Robert Hall's conclusion—arising from his polemic versus Mises—that "there is no index by which to decide that one savings rate is better than another . . . the decision is a political rather than an economic one."[6] What this amounts to is that no self-regulating mechanism can exist under socialist conditions that may lead the economy as the market does in capitalist free competition. Capitalist society is actually the only known society in which economy is the fundamental (though not exclusive) mediation area indispensable for the reproduction of society; the function of value fixing is to automatically sum up, mediate and concentrate every contradictory historical and moral element of bourgeois society, independently from men's will.[7]

What every soviet Marxist manual refers to as the "fundamental

5. Evsey Liberman, "Retorno al capitalismo?"; Evsey Liberman and Zinovi Zhitnitski, "La rentabilidad en el socialismo"; Yakov Liberman, "Los problemas teóricos." All these documents appeared in the monographic issue *Historia y Sociedad* centered on the USSR economic reform, 8, Mexico, Winter 1966.

6. R. L. Hall, *Essay on Economic Growth and Planning,* quoted by Dobb, *Welfare Economics,* p. 197.

7. This is why theories of non-capitalist production modes possessing a theoretical status similar to the theory of a capitalist mode of production cannot exist. See Raúl Olmedo, "El estatuto teórico de los modos de producción no capitalistas," *Historia y Sociedad,* 5, Mexico, 1975.

economic law of socialism" is not, in fact, a law, but a *political deed*.
The USSR Science Academy *Manual*, like all manuals, makes reference to Lenin's well-known quote, that socialism means "the
planned organization of the social process of production to ensure
the welfare and complete development of all members of society";
this is supposed to be the "fundamental economic law."[8] It is symptomatic that another "modernized" manual (adapted to Khrushchev's
economic reform) included the same quote by Lenin in the same
chapter concerning the fundamental economic law—although in
this case it is severed from the crucial concept of the "planned organization of the social process of production"[9] and that the word
"planned," which hardly appears in the text, is substituted by a
vague "advanced technique" used by the State. In this manual the
"fundamental economic law" is reduced to the subjective notion of
"welfare."

The crux of the problem, however, does not vary, since "the
decisive role in organizing the production, distribution and exchange of products in each of the stages during which socialism is
being built falls to the socialist State, led by the working class
party."[10] In other words, the economy is regulated and planned in
this given situation by extra-economic instances; namely, a political
force (the party)—embodied in the planning State—the activity of
which is oriented according to the interests of society as a whole. It
could be said that the fundamental economic law of socialism is the
absence of economic laws conceived in their classical sense, which
means that politics become the fundamental economic force. Here
the contradiction Mandel refers to between the *plan* and the *market*,
between what he calls a "non-capitalist" production and a "bourgeois" distribution makes its appearance.[11] What Mandel fails to
realize is that democratic, self-managing and popular interests are
expressed (despite limitations and deformations) by means of the
"bourgeois" market, whereas the logic of "non-capitalist" bureau-

8. Quoted in *Manual de economía política*, Academia de Ciencias de la URSS, Mexico:
Grijalbo, 1960, p. 455.

9. P. Nikitin, *Economía Política*, Moscow: Ediciones en Lenguas Extranjeras, 1961, p.
259.

10. *Ibid.*, p. 262.

11. See E. Mandel, *Tratado de economía marxista*, Mexico: Ediciones Era, 1969, vol. II, pp.
161ss.

cratic control is expressed in the plan. The outcome is that the market—and, consequently, price fixing—depends to a great extent on the correlation of political forces, which is why it cannot acquire the bourgeois character Mandel assigns to it. The fact that social wealth is distributed unequally[12] does not in itself endow the market with a bourgeois character; the determining fact is that this market cannot reach an automatism that would endow it with a capitalist character. The import and extension of the non-controlled and more or less tolerated parallel market express the people's supply needs that can be met only through illegal and informal ways that develop in the interstices of the rigid economic plans. This parallel market also operates as a frequently fundamental income complement for a large part of the population.

The centralized planning system has, on the other hand, stimulated the "industrial revolution" and the accelerated accumulation rhythms that exacted so much sacrifice and were the harsh tribute most socialist countries had to pay for their heritage of economic backwardness. The economic basis, by implication, undergoes accelerated and sudden changes not necessarily caused by "economic" reasons, whereas the State seems to enjoy an almost automatic stability as far as its reproduction is concerned.

The most dramatic example of a function "reversal" taken to extremes, in which politics become a rigid economic force, is that of the USSR during the Stalin period. The renowned Chief Administration of Corrective Labor Camps (the Gulag) was not solely a form of political repression. It seems that, at the end of the 30s, the Gulag was producing most of the country's timber, as well as important quantities of coal, gold and copper; it was also in charge of building great canals, highways and factories, especially in remote areas and in particularly harsh climates.[13] Both Ellenstein and Deutscher uphold that during this period approximately ten percent of the industrial work force was made up of prisoners who worked like slaves under the concentration camp system.[14] Although ten percent of the industrial work force is no trifling amount,

12. Between one to ten and one to twenty, according to information sources.
13. Roy Medvedev, *Le stalinisme*, Paris: Seuil, 1972, p. 443.
14. Ellenstein, *Histoire du phénomène stalinien*, p. 206.

particularly in political terms, it becomes secondary from the viewpoint of economic accumulation; it is nonetheless revealing as regards the transformation from political (and repressive) functions to
economic ones. Ellenstein describes the Stalinist State in the following terms:

> The State, the contemporary Leviathan, tends to absorb every-
> thing, devouring institutions which up until then were auton-
> omous, intervening in everybody's daily life, controlling
> everyone's each actions from birth to death. [15]

Stalinism brought about a brutal fusion of civil society and
State. The State's *loss of autonomy*—stimulated by the war, among
other things—was considerably accelerated. The latter statement
may well seem absurd, given the enormous arbitral power concentrated in Stalin himself. But the "relative autonomy" of the State—
used as a scientific concept, not as a descriptive trait (*i.e.* "personality cult")—implies a *separation* between State and society. That is,
society also gains autonomy vis-à-vis the State, although this was
obviously not the case under Stalinism, when many typically socialist tendencies were intensified in anomalous forms; generally speaking, the State in socialist countries—not unlike a hermaphrodite
devil—*must be everywhere* since economy cannot reproduce itself.
This implies a fundamental difference from capitalism as well as
from all precapitalist social forms; in the latter the presence of the
State imposed itself upon the reproduction of social relationships
instead of guaranteeing them, thereby transforming them *up to a
certain point,* so that it could reproduce itself as a relatively autonomous political entity. The social basis, however, continued to be a
relatively closed economy for domestic consumption, centered on a
community of artisans or farmers; in fact, the basis of society could
reproduce itself without the intervention of the extra-economic force
of the State. The latter, however, determined the concrete forms of
exploitation and surplus exaction. The eventual withdrawal of the
coercive political apparatus would have implied the end of exploitation without producing a disorganization of the economic basis of
society, [16] although when this occurred it brought about major conse-

15. *Ibid.,* p. 214.
16. Slavery might seem an exception, although this form of exploitation was never dominant, either in scale or extension, in the economy of ancient societies.

quences in the life of the smaller cities, in science, in religion, and in every spiritual activity that depended on economic surplus for its existence.

Capitalist exploitation, on the contrary, cannot be explained by the presence of extra-economic forces, although it depends for its survival on a State conveniently detached from the economy. The particularity of socialism, as a society in transition, is that its economy can only operate on the basis of the direct intervention of extra-economic forces (the workers' party, for instance) although—contrary to what occurs in precapitalist societies—this intervention acquires a compulsive character, without which the entire social edifice would collapse. The economy of socialist countries refuses to allow the State to contract or fall back significantly. A withdrawal of the State's planning functions would imply a collapse and a return to capitalism . . . or else a revolutionary leap towards a new communist society.

It has been rightly upheld that present-day socialism is "a production system in which the *labor surplus is politically determined* most succinctly, based on non-economic criteria (quite definitely, the survival of the State itself)."[17] Another analyst of socialist societies goes even further; according to him, not only the foundations of the exploitation mechanism are political by nature, but the true privileges obtained by those means are also by nature fundamentally political and cultural.[18] The implication is that despite unfair and unequal forms of wealth distribution, they conform a secondary situation that fails to explain or provide foundations for the penetrating logic underlying the socialist system; this is to say that a greater or lesser disparity concerning individual income does not substantially modify the actual roots of the process.[19]

The socialist revolution has, as it were, displaced the economy from the *place* it held in capitalist society; its new *place* is the State.

---

17. Istvan Mészáros, *Pouvoir et opposition,* p. 133.
18. Rudolf Bahro, *The Alternative in Eastern Europe,* London: NLB, 1979, p. 181–82.
19. This can be historically proved by observing the evolution of the income inequality in socialist countries; it is also comparatively demonstrated by studying the differences between more "egalitarian" countries such as China and less "egalitarian" ones such as the GDR. Even important changes in income distribution at an individual level do not affect the actual nature of the system.

Engels' insight into this "de-politization" process of the State apparatus is clear when he states that,

> the political State, and with it political authority, will disappear as a result of the coming social revolution; that is, public functions will lose their political character and be transformed into the simple administrative functions of watching over the true interests of society.[20]

Indeed, "social interests" in socialist countries have become "administrative functions." This, by the way, is expressed in the so-called economism of official soviet Marxism, and in the slogans where politics predominate over economy, characteristic of China's cultural revolution (a voluntaristic variation of economism).

According to supposedly social interests, the State is responsible for distributing and administrating the total social product into the seven parts Marx refers to in his *Critique of the Gotha Programme:* 1) cover for *replacement* of the means of production used up; 2) the additional portion for *expansion* of production; 3) *reserve* funds to provide against accidents and so on; 4) the general costs of *administration* not belonging to production (bureaucracy, the army); 5) costs intended for *the common satisfaction of needs* (schools, health services); 6) funds for those *unable to work* (the aged, the diseased); 7) finally, what remains after these deductions have been made is the worker's *salary*. Decisions as to how these deductions are used and how salaries are fixed crystalize in *administrative functions,* distinct from the State apparatus. As Marx pointed out, this transition situation contains the conditions for the circulation of commodities and, consequently, workers' salaries are proportionate to the work they contribute. The outcome is a situation of inequality: "Equal work and, consequently, equal participation in the social consumer fund, means, in fact, that some obtain more than others, some are richer than others."[21] Beyond a certain threshold of technological development, however, income differences become the expression of a new kind of inequality, that is, between those whose activity is linked to State areas of decision and the others, whose simple and compartmentalized work has no link with the conscious transformations of

20. F. Engels, "On Authority," in *Karl Marx,* p. 379.
21. *Karl Marx,* "Critique to the Gotha Programme," (2d ed.), p. 15.

society, but is simply exchanged for commodities. That is, a kind of work that enriches both the individual's consciousness and society, and another, compartmentalized and alienating, that impoverishes the individual mind while it enriches society. Rudolf Bahro defines these as psychologically productive work and psychologically unproductive work.

This polarized division, however, acquires complexity within a *continuum*. Its distribution can be analyzed according to administrative functions organized on the basis of total social product distribution. Indeed, the distribution of the total social product into seven parts, with its profound division between manual and intellectual labor, provokes the crystallization and, quite often too, the ankylosis of certain administrative functions. Moreover, this basis constitutes the seven major social groups, whose link and division determine socio-political dynamics to a great extent. During the crystallization process of economical-administrative functions, the seven cups that seem to brim over with accumulated social anger spill their plagues over socialist societies:

1) Functions linked to the replacement means of production nurture the growth of an extended layer of *technicians* and *scientists*.

2) Global decisions regarding the expansion of production are in the hands of *planners*.

3) Use of reserve funds, linked to politics of junctural oscillation production compensation, is in the hands of *enterprise managing directors*.[22]

4) Unproductive administration costs mainly support *civil and military bureaucracy*.

5) Costs concerning the satisfaction of common needs are mostly absorbed by education, culture and medicine; this kind of function is the basis for a large mass of *intellectuals*.

6) Funds equivalent to welfare costs and destined to support

---

22. How "reserve funds" are managed is very important, as this has traditionally enabled the unproductive accumulation of large quantities of equipment and budget, managed independently from the enterprise's profitability (it is not deduced from the profits, but comes from a State budget) to distribute "prizes" and to feed a parallel market. Reserve funds frequently stand for the negotiation power of enterprise managing directors regarding production plan assignation from above.

the disabled are absorbed by a *marginal population* (the elderly, the diseased).

7) Wages are, of course, shared out between all the groups; reference is made here, however, to the wages paid mainly to non-specialized or semi-specialized *productive workers*. Included here are the "profits" obtained by artisans and peasants organized in collective enterprises or who work on an individual basis, and who do not receive formal wages.

Resting on this social structure—only briefly sketched in here—is the State and party apparatus that establishes an internal distinction in each group according to a power hierarchy, at the pinnacle of which we find a political élite made up of individuals from *every* group: top-level technicians, scientists, and planners, top officials and militaries, top enterprise managers, high-ranking intellectuals, unproductive war or work-heroes (multilated but covered with medals), and union leaders. The logic behind this immense State apparatus lies in the administration of economical accumulation. Socialist accumulation, however, imposed by politics, lacks a logic of its own. In fact, although traditional concepts have been used as reference points, the division between "politics" and "economy" lacks meaning in socialist conditions; the intricate relationship between State administrative functions and production and distribution of social wealth requires a range of new concepts. Perhaps a new *political economy* has been constituted. The time has come to criticize it.

XVI The Extinction of the State Tower

(The Tower)

Emptied his bowl over the throne of the beast and its whole empire was plunged into darkness. Men were biting their tongues for pain.

Rev. 16:10

The struggle for democracy, whether under capitalist or socialist conditions, essentially seeks the self-government of people. There is no difference between bourgeois and socialist forms of democracy, although it is true that socialism—whether actually existing or theoretically designed—creates an entirely new situation as regards the insertion and situation of State and politics within the social structure, a situation whereby democracy can be extended to every sphere of life. However, experience proves that any attempt to "automatize" socialist economy is pointless—at least during the lengthy transition stage. The economy, as the product of a revolution whereby capitalist mercantile self-regulation is destroyed, is subjected to the political will—to the dictatorship of the proletariat. This situation not only implies a simple change or reversal of political and economical roles but, above all, a momentous change in the entire problem. The development of democracy in socialism no longer obeys the typical problems of bourgeois society arising from the relative *separation* between economy and politics, between civil society and State. This separation immediately introduce classic issues, such as juridical *equality* among those whose situation within the exploitation system makes them unequal; the issue of *freedom* linked to free market competition; and the issue of citizen *representation* in top political power instances (legislative and judicial power, parliament). Although these are juridical-political mechanisms characteristic of the modern capitalist State, their absence or precariousness in present-day socialist regimes is one of the greatest sources of conflict. In order to explore this situation, we could invert the question: Can a self-regulated democracy be achieved? Is political automation conceivable and applicable?

It is clear that centralized economic planning is at the root of the phenomena whereby the egalitarian practice of political freedom has been distorted, and popular representation mechanisms have been numbed. By its very nature, the vast centralized accumulation of economic, administrative, military and cultural functions in the new socialist State ankyloses "formal" political democracy, paradoxically hindered by the expansion of "economic" democracy. Strangely enough, socialist planning is fundamental both for the expansion of a true political democracy and a means of curbing it. The dream of a socialist economy, in which self-planning would occur almost spontaneously, consequently endowing political life with a liberal trend, has practically vanished. To a certain extent, the necessary condition for such a situation seems to lie in a major decentralization and a great impetus towards enterprise self-management. The State would then be similar to a tower watching over the process, instead of the direct economy administrator, as occurs in capitalist countries. As we have seen, however, there are formidable obstacles involved in the implementation of such a process.

The true self-management of society's productive sector, which might constitute itself as the objective basis for developing political democracy, *does not seem feasible during the transition process.* New value-price relationships prevent this, creating the foundations for the intervention of the political apparatus in the regulation of economy. On the other hand, the ideal image of an omnipresent State in the regulation of socio-economic democracy—which *represents* the majority of the people, administers *egalitarian justice,* and guarantees *political freedom*—is not produced in real life in socialist countries; this ideal image harbors a substantial contradiction between State logic linked to economic accumulation and the logic of political democracy. The only way to overcome this contradiction is to implement new autonomous and self-reproducing forms of political democracy without the intervention of human will, however paradoxical this may seem. It is obvious that if this is to occur, shaping actual laws according to a democratic model is not enough, since its automatic functioning requires certain objective conditions.

At this stage, we could explore a new alternative: how would a socialist society operate in which a *separation* between economic democracy processes and political democracy mechanisms were to materialize? In this situation—although the global condition of political democracy would be socialist planning—its real, objective basis would not be determined by the democratic regulation of material production. This starting point—not merely for reflection but also for struggle—can be very interesting, since experience has shown that the *fusion* of economic and political democracy (creating a so-called true democracy) has the effect of impoverishing political democracy.

The point, however, is not merely to reproduce within a socialist context a democratic formalism such as that established in certain capitalist countries with liberal regimes. Even in a centralized and planned economy, political democracy can become a mere formalism when confronted with the enormous power concentrated in the State apparatus, as occurs in capitalist countries confronted with the strength of major monopolies and that of the ruling class. However, the so-called *formal character* of democracy conceals precious elements that constitute, in fact, a triumph for the popular mass. One of these elements is, precisely, the appreciation that democracy can *only* function efficiently for the mass of the people *if* it operates relatively *separated* from the processes of social and economic domination. One might say that its condition of existence is its "formalism." Agnès Heller is right in asserting that,

> all those who would like to substitute formal democracy for what they call true democracy, that unites State and society again in a global and indistinct group, are by this very fact renouncing democracy.[1]

It is nonetheless hardly satisfactory to prove that political democracy can only *truly* operate insofar as it is *formally* constituted, that is, separated from society. The latter must, in turn, ensure the *conditions* for the *survival* of democracy, since it does not in itself contain them. Democracy thereby derives its formal character, which is to say that on its own it "leaves problems concerning the structural organization of society unsolved."[2] This is why democracy adapts itself to entirely dissimilar social and economic systems; although the adaptation indicates that society has in some way organized mechanisms guaranteeing its survival for a given period. The capitalism-democracy relationship has been carefully studied from

1. Agnès Heller, "El porvenir de la democracia socialista," *Historia y Sociedad,* n. 22, Mexico, 1980.
2. *Ibid.*

very different angles, showing, in general terms, that the relatively automatic regulation of production and market provides the conditions for the survival of the democratic government; it is also a fact that the development of major transnational monopolies, capable of overcoming the typical processes of free competition capitalism, tends to undermine the very foundations of democracy.

Under socialist conditions—that is, of transition—the guarantees for the survival of democracy must be situated within the initially incipient and later accelerated development of the *extinction of the State*. In other words, the basis of these guarantees cannot be found in the new centralizing and planning functions that, contrariwise, tend to strengthen the State. Democracy itself is, at bottom, nothing but the extinction of the State and the suppression of social class, which is why it ignores these classes. If democracy is the government of people by the people, this implies—at least theoretically and embryonically—the suppression of social classes and the class-based State. During the period of socialist transition, however, the State apparatus gathers strength, expanding considerably, thanks to the new regulation functions assigned by the revolution to the productive process to guarantee the destruction of capitalist production relationships. It has been stated that, once the initial economic development objectives are reached, the only way to achieve democracy lies in the expansion of a self-managing, decentralized and autonomous production system. Generally speaking, this is true. However, an economism-oriented conception of self-management has predominated, thus establishing an exceedingly direct and mechanical relationship between the economic autonomy of enterprises and the functioning of democracy. The great difficulties arising from the implementation of a new self-managing and self-regulated economy have already been discussed; that of the greatest consequence, though, is the exact reproduction of the classic capitalist model in designing a process whereby political democracy should naturally follow from economic democracy. The truth is that even in the classic capitalist model, democracy is by no means derived from economy; instead, it develops and adapts to bourgeois society on the basis of an intense and prolonged popular struggle. Democracy has never issued normally, naturally and logically from capitalist production and market laws.

The same occurs under socialist conditions: political democracy does not emerge spontaneously from self-management; much less so from central economic plans. The socialist forms of self-management—usually weak at the outset—are not the most important sign of the extinction of the State, which begins with socialism, although perhaps only as an unsatisfied need. The signs of this extinction appear mainly in areas that enable its reproduction as a dominating entity. These State reproduction mechanisms—economic and political by nature, but mainly cultural and ideological—are constituted in what I have termed *mediation structures*. Any democratizing impetus in these structures is a symptom of the State's difficulties to reproduce itself. This becomes very clear in socialist States where, given the fusion between politics and economy, all forms of advanced political democratization is experienced as an attempt against the process of socialist accumulation. Strictly speaking, however, this situation is the outcome of the concrete historical form within which socialist countries have been conformed. The subsequent evolution of socialism—although it may probably undergo a profound revolutionary crisis—is not blindly determined by the omnipresence of the State. The crisis of the socialist State's mediating or legitimizing structures may unleash new forms of democratic struggle.

In conditions of block confrontation and balance at an international scale, and of great economic backwardness in socialist countries, it was nonetheless possible to advance towards the extinction of the State without weakening it. Expressed in terms of a struggle, it could be regarded as a case of *strategic* weakening and *tactical* strengthening of the State both in existing socialist countries and where revolutions are geared towards a socialist democracy. This implies that the mechanisms of electoral procedure, together with the guarantees of free expression and organization, the disappearance of the secret political police, civil rights, and multi-party struggle—no matter what their juridical mode—require for their survival the support and protection from *a complete autonomy and self-management of not directly productive major activities* (education, culture, science, health services, mass media, party cadre structure). In this dream, the State would thus become a sort of technocratic-administrative eggshell that would regulate the economical system and be endowed with a relatively autonomous parliamentary-like political-legislative extension. This would ensure the existence of democratic forms within the State and guarantee the autonomous existence of the socio-cultural sector. The purpose of this kind of struggle process—the embryo of which can be already observed in socialist countries—is to seize a sizable part of mediation structures from the State, the ones now securing its reproduction as an apparatus of domination and control.

Under these conditions, the State—in order to ensure its reproduction—will have to resort to a new kind of autonomous democracy belt managing the main economically non-productive scientific and political-cultural functions. All this could be translated into the implementation of three power forms: the *economic-administrative power,* in charge of planning the productive sector and centralized to a greater or lesser extent according to the degree of development; the *political-legislative power,* responsible for the elaboration of national and international politics; and the *cultural-scientific power,* autonomous and governed by its own mechanisms of function and position election, in whose hands both culture and scientific research would lie, together with the organization of the common satisfaction of needs, such as education, public health services, leisure and mass media. Of course, a non-repressive power that is independent, endowed with representative instances and watched over by civil society must exist.

A situation such as that briefly described would be an important step towards the strategic weakening of the State, as it would be castrated since the conditions for its reproduction would not be self-contained. A tactical strengthening would occur simultaneously, simply because its capacity for a balanced diversified development would have favorable repercussions on the international relations of a democratic socialist State of this kind. The alternative for socialism proposed and analyzed by Rudolf Bahro—centered on the need for a cultural revolution—corresponds to the above-mentioned proposals. I have merely found it worthwhile to stimulate a reflection on the essential conditions required for the irreversible extinction of the State. Bahro's book, *The Alternative,* proves that socialist countries have the necessary social bases and forces to open the doors to a new path leading towards democracy.

It is important to bear in mind that I am dealing here with possible democratic alternatives for *a transition process;* the fight would center on a two-power division (economic and political) of the State, which is surrounded—and to a great extent permanently besieged—by what in fact would be a popular cultural-scientific *counter-power.* Transitional democratic socialism must solve the classical problems of juridical equality among unequals, of individual freedom in the choice of paths offered to the members of an as yet unfair society, and of the people's representation in political instances. It also contains, however, entirely new elements, such as the real autonomy of that immense area where artistic, scientific and ideological elements are engendered, and where education, leisure, communication and social medicine are organized. This autonomy implies, in fact, and for the very first time in history, a situation wherein the State depends on *massive forces organized extra-economically and extra-politically,* the dynamics of which begin to obey norms of an advanced communist society utopia. Moreover, the parallel and autonomous organization of these forces provides a powerful guarantee that so-called formal democracy will become a true democratic form.

XVII The Oligarchy of the Martyrs

(The Stars)

"The waters you saw, beside which the prostitute was sitting, are all the peoples, the populations, the nations and the languages."

Rev. 17:15

It is curious that two writers so distant in time and ideas as Engels and D. H. Lawrence should have concurred in their appreciation on the relationship between primitive Christianity and modern socialism. Engels wrote that Renan was absolutely right in asserting that "in order to have an idea of early Christian communities, one need only observe a local association of the International Workers' Association."[1] D. H. Lawrence, on the other hand, in his superb essay on the Book of Revelation, developed the idea of the existence of a profound link between popular primitive religion and the congregationalist universe of North Midland miners gathered in Methodist chapels.[2]

Let us take a look at some aspects of this convergence. According to Engels, primitive Christianity fed on the dissolution of the ancient world.

> At that time, in Rome and Greece, and even more so in Asia Minor, Syria and Egypt, it was unquestionably accepted and completed with the pious falsehoods of an insolent quackery, a nonsensical mingling of the crasser superstitions from all countries, in which thaumaturgy, convulsions, visions, fortune telling, alchemy and other occult sorceries fulfilled an important role.[3]

Engels sums up the adventures of an early Christian prophet, Peregrinus, whom he compares to socialist prophets like Albrecht, Kuhlmann and Weitling, those "archdemocratic and egalitarian" disciples were taken in by the vague promises of a "new world"

---

1. F. Engels, "Sobre la historia del cristianismo primitivo," *Historia y Sociedad*, n. 7, Mexico, 1975, p. 27.
2. D. H. Lawrence, *Apocalypse*, New York: Viking Press, 1982.
3. Engels, "Sobre la historia," p. 32.

announced by authoritarian communist evangelists of human eman-
cipation. Engels wrote:

> And in the same way there flock to the worker's party of all
> countries those elements which have nothing to expect from
> the official world or are expelled from it, such as those oppos-
> ing vaccination, vegetarians, witch-doctor medicine partisans,
> preachers of dissident congregations deserted by their flock,
> authors of new theories on the origin of the world, unfortunate
> or unsuccessful inventors, victims of real or imaginary set-
> backs, honest imbeciles and insolent impostors; the same
> thing happened with the Christians. All the elements emanci-
> pated by the process of dissolution of the ancient world were
> added, one after the other, to Christianity's circle of gravita-
> tion. . . . There was no known exaltation, extravagance, base-
> ness or knavery that was not produced among the young
> Christian communists.[4]

Engels finds in the New Testament's Book of Revelation, the
most complete expression of early Christian communist thought.

For D. H. Lawrence, the Book of Revelation expressed the
feelings and ideas of the weak and pseudo-meek mass bent on de-
stroying all pagan *might* so that *authority* and *power* could take its
place: "it is the Christianity of the middling masses, this Christianity of the Apocalypse."[5] D. H. Lawrence asks: "How can the
anti-power masses, above all the great middling masses, ever take a
king who is more than a thing of ridicule or pathos? The Apocalypse
has been running for nearly two thousand years: the hidden side of
Christianity: and its work is nearly done."[6] In fact, Lawrence says
that "when you start to teach individual self-realization to the great
masses of people, who when all is said and done are only *fragmentary*
beings, *incapable* of whole individuality, you end by making them
all envious, grudging spiteful creatures."[7]

D. H. Lawrence realized that the Book of Revelation is one of
the most ancient texts on State theory. John of Patmos—obviously
not the same John of the gospels—formulated the Christian theory

4. *Ibid.*, p. 30.
5. D. H. Lawrence, *Apocalypse*, p. 104.
6. *Ibid.*, p. 14.
7. *Ibid.*, p. 105.

of the State in Revelation: this viewpoint "entails the destruction of the whole world, and the reign of saints in ultimate bodiless glory. Or it entails the destruction of all earthly power, and the rule of an oligarchy of martyrs (the Millennium)."[8] Next Lawrence asserts that "the oligarchy of martyrs began with Lenin," whom he has previously defined as "a great evil saint who believes in the utter destruction of power" since every saint becomes evil from the moment they touch upon the collective self of man.[9]

The problem posed by Lawrence and Engels, each in their own way, is that of discovering the profound links between certain ancient religious forms with popular roots and the phenomenon of the modern popular socialist struggle. Is this not the same problem facing modern Marxists who attempt to understand, for instance, the apparent revival of despotic "oriental" forms in present day socialist systems? In more general terms, we are up against the need to explain the centuries-old persistence of certain myths and symbols illustrating both ancient and modern mechanisms that assist the reproduction of political power and the struggle against domination. In a sense it is the same problem Freud tackled in his classic studies on totemism and on the role played by Moses in the origins of monotheistic religion. Freud concluded that the scientific explanation behind the persistence of ancient popular traditions in the creation of a national character—and the fact that different peoples share the same symbols—can only be understood if peoples and masses are analyzed as if they were neurotic individuals.[10] Freud supports his thesis, according to which the mechanism of the *symbolic substitution* of one object for another—characteristic of individual psychology—operates similarly among the masses and peoples, by means of the following argument: "A tradition solely founded on verbal transmissions could not have a coercive character typical of religious phenomena."[11] As is well known, Freud's starting point in understanding monotheistic religion is the *original death of the father*, as a precocious trauma unleashing defense mechanisms, latency and

---

8. *Ibid.*, p. 106.
9. *Ibid.*, p. 13–14.
10. S. Freud, *Der Mann Moses un die Monotheistische Religion*, Amsterdam: Verlag Allert de Lange, 1939, p. 117.
11. *Ibid.*, p. 119.

—finally—the explosion of a neurotic process. Wilhelm Reich lived and died obsessed by this very problem of how to fathom the persistence of popular mass coercion, obedience, acceptance and tolerance mechanisms. After witnessing a huge popular demonstration in Austria, characterized by bloody police repression, Reich wrote:

> I was astonished at the meekness of the population. The multitude was so strong that it could have literally torn the few policemen to pieces. But there was a calm, almost joyful, atmosphere. And the police were able to circulate unarmed in the multitude, even though citizens were being murdered like rabbits nearby. I could not understand it. Why did the multitude look on, doing nothing, absolutely nothing, to stop the slaughter? Where was the *sadism of the masses?*[12]

These events, which occurred in 1927, prompted Reich to criticize Freud's theses on mass psychology which he found unsatisfactory because they interpreted the identification with the leader and the loss of individual personality as an eternal phenomenon rooted in biological laws.

How are obedience impulses transmitted? How can traditions about the acceptance of coercion be explained? What is their origin? Engels and Lawrence were not far off the track when they sought for an answer in the Book of Revelation, as the obedience tradition of a people or culture does not lie in the unconscious transmission of an ancient ideological structure (originated, for instance, in the "death of the father"), but in the capacity acquired by certain sociopolitical structures—mainly during transition periods—to "transfer" or "displace" profound contradictions towards mediation areas. To continue the Freudian metaphors, we could say that this mediation structure's "symbolic material" is derived from the (partly "unconscious") "cultural tradition," and that its similarity with mediations in other cultures derives from its close link with the reproduction mechanism of society which operates by continually engendering mediation structures. Transition periods—during which huge masses of the population are compelled to transit from one world to another and experience situations involving dramatic displacements and

---

12. *People in Trouble*, p. 10, quoted by Luigi de Marchi, *Wilhelm Reich, biografía de una idea*, Barcelona: Península, 1974, p. 60.

marginality (or "anomia," as Durkheim would say)—stimulate the appearance of institutions, organizations and ideologies capable of "translating" the old to the new socio-cultural language. Mediation structures are typical creatures of transition processes, in which the instability of a predominating cultural, political and social heterogeneity presses masses of individuals (highly fragmented in themselves) to engender all kinds of structures and ideas that conceal, under an exotic appearance, a mediating mechanism capable of adapting or translating the peculiar contradictory terms of the variegated nature of a society in transition.

The Book of Revelation is one of the most ancient examples of mediation in Western culture. This is why its symbolism is so alive today. In the Book of Revelation, as in any mediating structure, we have a typical articulated duality of two powers or elements in which the one apparently destined to dominate engenders its opposite. This engendering and manipulation of adverse power is produced not unlike the paradoxical assimilation of popular pagan elements which establish the new cult's objective and historical foundations; the "symbolic substitution" or "displacement" operates here, concealed behind "translation" mechanisms of ancient cultural symbols. Only a transition—and, consequently, dissolution—process of the ancient world (or of the *ancien régime*) prompts the objective popular basis of the new ideology to be formed by that heterogeneous multitude of elements inducing the typical confusion of sects, prophets, spirit of sacrifice, quackery and bellicose ardor of the popular mass, integrated by fragmentary beings referred to by Lawrence and Engels.

In Revelation the two major contradictory powers are embodied in the *prostitute of Babylon* and the *Lamb*, in the kingdom of the Beast and the Kingdom of God. The Lamb's meekness—as well as that of the docile martyrs whom it represents—can only be attained in the war waged against the pagan mass. Engels has said that, "the saints and martyrs are avenged by the destruction of Babylon, of the great prostitute and all her partisans, which is to say the great majority of men."[13] Indeed, the cult to the great prostitute of Babylon described in every appetizing detail in Revelation has its origins in

13. Engels, "Sobre la historia," p. 39.

one of Asia Minor's most ancient and popular cults. It is a known fact that in ancient Babylon every woman, once in her lifetime, had to give herself up to a stranger at the temple of Mylitta and dedicate to the goddess the wages earned by this sanctified harlotry. The same custom prevailed in Heliopolis, Syria, where every maiden had to prostitute herself to a stranger at the temple of Astarte. Religious prostitution was part of a fertility cult that extended through most of Asia Minor. Frazer has carried out a thorough research concerning these cults in which a great Mother Goddess is invariably worshipped.

> That associated with her was a lover, or rather series of lovers, divine yet mortal, with whom she mated year by year, their commerce being deemed essential to the propagation of animals and plants, each in their several kind . . . and further, that the fabulous union of the divine pair was simulated and, as it were, multiplied on earth by the real, though temporary, union of the human sexes at the sanctuary of the goddess for the sake of thereby ensuring the fruitfulness of the ground and the increase of man and beast.[14]

This rich and heterogenous pagan religion is taken up by the author of Revelation but is adapted in such a way that the great fertility goddess is regarded mainly as the embodiment of evil in the great prostitute of Babylon and fleetingly, as the mother of the Lamb. In this sense, the great prostitute of Babylon not only represents the Roman empire, but all the pagan mass subjected by Rome.

The duality of powers is one of the characteristics which those specialized in the study of the Book of Revelation have pointed out for a long time now. Allo has written that,

> The first thread is what I will call, if you want, the law of the perpetuation of antithesis. . . . Is there at bottom anything else but the opposition of two societies, of two cities as St. Augustine would say, that of the friends of God, the true Jerusalem governed by the Lamb, and that of their enemies, Babylon, dominated by the Dragon?[15]

14. James G. Frazer, *The Golden Bough: A Study in Magic and Religion*, New York: The Macmillan Company, 1947, p. 331.
15. Allo, *L'Apocalypse*, Paris: Études Bibliques, 1921, LXXVI.

Another specialist in biblical studies has pointed out that in Revelation "John opposed in a spirited antithesis the order of the Lamb to that of the Beast . . . the Christian order he upholds is exactly opposite to the pagan order he knows and fights against; by means of the first we can guess at the second, and in its transparency, the terrible pair of the imperial cult associated with the Mother of Gods can be seen" (he is referring to the cults to Domitian and Cybele.)[16]

What is interesting about Revelation is the way in which the wealth of popular pagan thought is inserted into a dialectical apparatus capable of transforming the beauty and sensuality of the ancient mother earth myth into a harmful order, over the ruins of which the new Christian order must build that represented by the Lamb. D. H. Lawrence captured this dialectical moment with great lucidity when he stated that,

> only the great whore of Babylon rises rather splendid, sitting in her purple and scarlet and upon her scarlet beast. She is the Magna Mater in malefic aspect, clothed in the colors of the angry sun, and throned upon the red dragon of the cosmic power. Splendid she sits, and splendid is her Babylon. How the late apocalyptists love mouthing out all about the gold and silver and cinnamon of evil Babylon. How they *want* them all! How they *envy* Babylon her splendor, envy, envy! How they love destroying it all. The harlot sits magnificent with her golden cup of the wine of sensual pleasure in her hand. How the apocalyptists would have loved to drink out of her cup! And since they could not, how they loved smashing it![17]

Regarding this very issue, Engels points out that the Book of Revelation reflects the conflict between Christian Jews and converted pagans. Jewish orthodoxy—which looked with disgust upon sexual freedom and the ingestion of meat from pagan sacrifices—was in this sense violently opposed to the non-Jewish popular customs young Christians of pagan origins brought with them to the sect. For this reason the new order of the Lamb is an entirely asexual

16. P. Touilleux, *L'Apocalypse et les cultes de Domitien et de Cybèle*, Paris: Librairie Orientaliste Paul Geuthner, 1935, p. 99.
17. D. H. Lawrence, *Apocalypse*, p. 76–77.

universe; as Engels pointed out, "in this heaven of John's, there is not a single woman."[18] Likewise, there was an absence of sensuality and pleasure in the Stalinist ideal; and while Marxist manuals of the period criticized capitalism, they were distilling the same kind of envy experienced by the authors of Revelation.

Thus the war waged against the popular pagan world was also an internal war resolved in Revelation by means of a crushing and imaginary dialectical apparatus recreating Evil almost permanently so as to revitalize faith in the future kingdom of Good, embodied in the decapitated Lamb. This image (and that of the shepherd, which appears elsewhere in the Bible) also has ancient roots, like those of the myth of the great prostitute of Babylon. It is known that the Asian cult to the great mother goddess of fertility developed in Phrygia as the worship of the goddess Cybele. According to the legend, Cybele's lover was a beautiful and young shepherd called Attis, who was her son. One of the legend's versions has it that Attis died when he unmanned himself under a pine-tree, where he bled to death. It was believed that after his death, Attis was changed into a pine-tree. The ancient Phrygian cult to the fertility goddess Cybele expanded together with the worship of Attis, the god-shepherd who was the Great Goddess's son and lover. The symbol frequently used to represent this god was a lamb's head, together with the Phrygian cap. The ritual involving the worship of Attis included the sacrifice of a lamb and most probably the mutilation of its genitals, representing the god's castration under a pine-tree. It is probable that the cult to Attis had its origin in the worship of a mythical lamb among Phrygian shepherd tribes inhabiting the Anatolia plains; later on, the god's figure was humanized by adopting the figure of a shepherd surrounded by his flock, symbolized by the lamb.

Thus the meekness which was attributed to the kingdom of God, of the New Jerusalem, is linked to the historical origin of the symbolism used in Revelation, namely the castrated shepherd and his flock.

The Asian cult to Cybele was adopted by the Romans in 204 B.C. Later on, Emperor Claudius adopted this Phrygian cult to the

18. Engels, "Sobre la historia," p. 35.

sacred tree as the official State religion; every year Rome celebrated the great spring festival of Cybele and Attis. Frazer says:

> Certainly the Romans were familiar with the Galli, the emasculated priests of Attis, before the close of the Republic. These unsexed beings, in their Oriental costume, with little images suspended on their breasts, appear to have been a familiar sight in the streets of Rome, which they traversed in procession carrying the image of the goddess and chanting their hymns to the music of cymbals and tambourines, flutes and horns, while the people, impressed by the fantastic show and moved by the wild strains, flung showers of roses. [19]

The great spring festival culminated on the third day (March 24, known as the "Day of Blood") in a ceremony in which, stirred by the music, the priests of Attis, frenetically dancing around the sacred tree, gashed their bodies and arms in order to bespatter the altar and the sacred tree with their blood. It seems that the same day the novices castrated themselves, offering their severed members to the goddess. "These broken instruments of fertility," writes Frazer, "were afterwards reverently wrapped up and buried in the earth or in subterranean chambers sacred to Cybele". [20]

Frazer established a relationship between this rite and the fact that many other Asian fertility goddesses were also served by eunuch priests; the reception of their divine lovers' masculine attributes engendered a life-giving energy which the goddess then transmitted to the world.

In writing his Revelation, John of Patmos must have adopted the ancient popular symbolism of Phrygian origin, although he reversed the roles, since the secondary eunuch god in this case dethrones his mother and lover, the great Asian fertility goddess, embodying in her all evil and sin. This is why the God-Lamb kingdom he conceived could be nothing but an oligarchy of eunuch-martyrs imposed on the great mass of sinners. The dream of total and omnipresent power was based on the assimilation, reversal and displacement of popular traditions belonging to an immense

---

19. Frazer, *Golden Bough*, p. 348.
20. *Ibid.*, p. 349.

"marginal" mass (marginal as regards the ancient world in dissolution). Stalinism in a way also created an apocalyptic apparatus which managed to absorb old pagan Marxism and transform it into the enemy's creature to be resisted; the actual battle engendered the conditions for the reproduction of a new ideology that consolidated the despotic power of socialism's eunuch-martyrs, those enlightened bureaucrats that became the authors of a new Revelation which, as Engels put it, aroused

> the comrades to an energetic, resolute and courageous propaganda of their faith vis-à-vis their adversaries, and the ceaseless struggle against the enemy, whether within or without.

The dogmatic letters John of Patmos addressed to the churches, as Engels concludes, "could well have been written by an enthusiast of the International, without being a prophet."[21] There is no doubt, however, that it is the modern industrial and capitalist society which reproduces most faithfully the image of a homogeneous society likened to a flock of sinners among whom is extended the omnipresent power of the Lamb—that is to say, of the capital.

---

21. Engels, "Sobre la historia," p. 36.

XVIII The Lunatic Fringe

(The Moon)

"Babylon has fallen, Babylon the Great has fallen, and has become the haunt of devils and a lodging for every foul spirit and dirty, loathsome bird."

Rev. 18:2

Modern anthropology has discovered misbehavior patterns in every society; it is as if society were to say, "don't do this, but if you do, do it this way."[1] Research on the "deviation" mechanisms of cultural norms has proved the universality of this phenomenon, although their interpretation frequently falls into a narrow psychologism limited to the analysis of the deviated individual's behavior, without even attempting to establish the nature of the social models in relation to which society pre-structures individual or collective misbehavior. This is what Georges Devereux reproaches Ralph Linton for.[2] Devereux, founder of modern ethnopsychiatry, has shown that there are "antisocial social values which enable the individual to be antisocial in a socially approved and sometimes even prestigious way."[3] Western culture offers a whole set of examples of such antisocial forms of behavior. We have already referred to the celebrated case of Peregrinus, narrated by Lucian, a member of the sect of cynics, who became a Christian and ended by creating his own religious form. Peregrinus masturbated publicly, was tortured for adultery during his youth in Armenia, and ended his days by committing a dramatic suicide during an olympic festival, a self-immolation publicly announced with anticipation to ensure the success of the show: he cremated himself on the Olympic fire in 165.

The classical example in ethnological studies of a socially approved deviation is that of the *berdaches* of the Mojave tribe. When a man considered himself incapable of becoming a warrior—the highest ideal among this war-loving tribe—he became a *berdache*. He would dress like a woman and assume female chores; those who were homosexual married another man. Mojave society condoned and

1. Ralph Linton, *The Study of Man: An Introduction*, New York: Appleton Century Co., Inc., 1936.
2. G. Devereux, *Essais d'ethnopsychiatrie générale*, Paris: Gallimard, 1977, p. 34.
3. *Ibid.*, p. 36.

accepted the *berdache* far more readily than a warrior who proved to be a failure. There are countless examples of socially and culturally determined forms of abnormal behavior. Paraphrasing Linton, Devereux concludes that society seems to provide the following directions: "be careful you don't become mad, but if you do, behave in such or such a way."[4] Psychoanalysts are familiar with this phenomenon. Early analysts encountered symptom neurosis in general, whereas they found patients during the 30s suffering mostly from character neurosis, unlike the alterations related to the sense of identity prevalent nowadays. It is obvious that in the United States the changes in the makeup of "the lunatic fringe" as it is popularly called (referring to groups of eccentrics living on the "margin" of society) are not due to mechanisms which individual psychopathology can explain. During the Mahoma period, epilepsy was the typical disorder among the Arabs; since epilepsy was considered a manifestation of divinity, military leaders would fake a seizure the night before a battle to stimulate their troops. We shall never know, says Devereux, whether Mahoma's famous epilepsy was real or feigned. The list of ethnically-rooted mental disorders is endless; well-known cases are the *latah* and *amok* among the Malayans, the *berserk* among the ancient Scandinavians, the *imu* among the Ainus, the *windigo* among Canada's Algonquins, the Crazy-dog-that-wants-to-die syndrome among the Crow Indians and the *berdaches* among the Mojaves.

The conclusion reached by ethnopsychiatrists is that each culture and society offer defense mechanisms and a range of symptoms which enable anguish to be fixed and conflicts induced by mental traumatisms and disorders to be confronted.[5] These symptoms differ entirely from those of a diseased individual who "improvises" defense mechanisms according to his idiosyncratic peculiarities (originating, of course, in the material provided by the environment, without fulfilling, however, a socially symptomatic function). Devereux has classified mental non-idiosyncratic disorders into three kinds: ethnical disorders, sacred disorders and typical disorders.

In ethnical disorders, symptoms and defense mechanisms are

4. *Ibid.*, p. 39.
5. *Ibid.*, p. 73.

elaborated *as such* by a given culture, and manifested by means of the above-mentioned antisocial patterns of behavior.

Sacred disorders—shamanism is the clearest example—imply the presence of neurosis in the ethnic segment of an individual's unconscious. Devereux offers a simple illustration by means of the following example:

> For the Ute tribe, one thing is to believe that the shaman harbors within an Homunculus-Devourer-of-Evil, and an entirely different thing is that the Ute shaman himself should feel the presence of that Homunculus. To confuse one with the other is equivalent to the rejection of the difference between what is sociological and what psychological. In brief, the shaman is not a neurotic because he *participates* in the *beliefs* of his tribe; he is neurotic because in *his* particular case, and *only* in his case, this *belief* is transformed, for neurotic reasons, in a subjective experience, albeit culturally structured, of a hallucinatory kind.[6]

Finally, there are typical disorders, defined according to the kind of society which produces them (urban, industrial, agrarian, and so on).

Ethnopsychiatric studies—regardless of the actual psychological problems they pose—allow for the discussion of the fundamental theme: the reproduction of the unity of a global social body. Functionalist and structuralist oriented anthropological interpretations conclude that mental disturbances and disorders are "functional" as regards global society; rather than being actual illnesses or anomalies, they fulfill a precise cultural function. Indeed, it seems that the culture itself provides or determines the symptoms and defense mechanisms that enable the individual to behave antisocially in a socially acceptable way. As François Laplantine puts it:

> Mental illness is never nonsensical, which would remit us to descriptions in a bestiary. It is a counter-sense or, more exactly, another possible sense regarding what a given society defines as a primary sense. It cannot structurally be called abnormal except insofar as it moves away from the norm culturally shared by most members in a society, and thus

---

6. *Ibid.*, p. 25.

conforms to *other* norms that also form part of a total system which provides behavior models that, although marginal, are not less conventional and acceptable for the group as a whole.[7]

Ethnic disorder *is* an antibehavior pattern; sacred disorder *is manifested* as a cultural structure and the typical disorder *expresses* a given social state. Such assertions confine us to the typical formulations of cultural relativism espoused by functionalist and structuralist thought. The crux of the matter is that despite the indisputable fact that symptom and defense mechanisms are a constituent and functional part of the social body, this by no means cancels the possibility that they express an abnormal and diseased situation.

The question is where the "abnormal" and "diseased" lies in a society and what such concepts conceal. We are faced here with two contradictory alternatives as regards interpretation: the functionalists, culturalists and behaviorists would say that the abnormal marginal phenomenon is a constituent of a *coherent group* of social and cultural institutions. We could say, on the other hand, that the manifestation of coherence is a process that conceals, even as it expresses, the *contradictions* (incoherences) of global society. The first explanation is incapable of understanding the evolution—and therefore the extinction—of a system of social and cultural relations.

If we break away from traditional definitions, we must acknowledge that nothing can appear as radically "abnormal" in a society save the processes of *extinction* of those conditions that help to reproduce it as a socio-cultural unity. As Devereux's ethnopsychiatric essays reveal, he has realized this and provided the following non-functionalist solution:

> Every society comprises not merely "functional" aspects by means of which it affirms and maintains its integrity, but also a certain amount of beliefs, dogmas and tendencies that contradict, deny or undermine not only the group's essential operations and structures, but their very existence at times.[8]

We could say that every society has a death-wound that secretes these socially conditioned ideal antisocial types that poison

---

7. *L'étnopsychiatrie*, Paris: Editions Universitaires, 1973, p. 67.
8. Devereux, *Essais*, p. 34.

the social body. Even as society itself produces the poison which is to destroy it, it also engenders processes whereby the poison itself is temporarily "functional." Every society's mortal wound is the social struggle in its myriad manifestations. Devereux provides revealing examples; various forms of extreme idealism which deny any reality to the world of the senses or conceive it as radically sinful have induced "deviated" behavior exhibited by saints, hermits, and yogis, whose initial attempt against the actual survival of society simultaneously fulfills an integrating religious "function." Medieval theologians—inspired in St. Augustine's ideal of the City of God—conceived of all earthly rule as evil by definition, thus condemning all economic and social activity destined to the survival of society. This contempt of the earthly world is a curious variation on the contempt felt by the ruling class towards the exploited pariahs, tainted by performing useful tasks. History gives us many other examples of how the social conflict creates an evidently irrational and self-destructive (and consequently non-functional) ideology; at the same time, however, those assailed by the "disease"—prophets, saints, martyrs—fulfill a function by maintaining and integrating "normal" social values. Devereux provides another, rather beautiful, example concerning this conflict present in Emperor Marcus Aurelius's *Meditations*. Even though he carried out his imperial duties efficiently, he never ceased to regard them with contempt, seeing in them an obstacle to his Stoic ideal. As Devereux says,

> Since it is quite evident that society's contempt towards those operations most useful to it and towards those who fulfill them is a manifestation of its self-destructive tendencies, I maintain that the Stoicism of Marcus Aurelius is almost in itself enough to explain the decline and fall of the Roman Empire.[9]

This is the kind of phenomena that although initially related to self-destructive tendencies, is conveyed, under certain conditions, to "functional" areas of society. There are many ways in which conflictive and contradictory elements are conveyed or transferred to mediating zones. The examples I have already provided refer to the

9. *Ibid.*, p. 35.

irrational ideology of the ruling class as an expression of self-destructive tendencies. The dominated classes create, however, the most destructive forms of thought and action; forms which are also transferred under certain conditions, thereby fulfilling mediating functions. In actual fact, the mediation structures nurtured by the popular masses are the most enduring and efficient of all.

XIX Flitcraft's Parable or the Adventures of Overdetermination

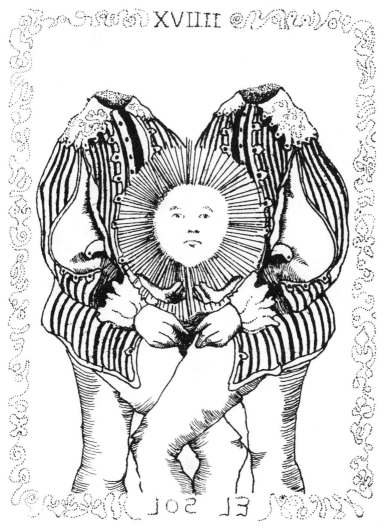

(The Sun)

But the beast was taken prisoner, together with the false prophet. . . . These two were thrown alive into the fiery lake of burning sulphur.

Rev. 19:20

I have insisted that the simple assertion that economic contradictions determine political and cultural life *in the last instance* fails to offer an adequate explanation as to the conditions under which global society is reproduced; it prevents us, moreover, from discovering those elements that endow it with a specific unity and coherence. The problem, posed with great precision by Althusser, is as follows: how is one to explain the determination of a structure's internal elements (*i.e.* that of the economic structure), as well as their inter-relationship? What concept might enable us to conceive a relation between two structures, one of them subordinate to the other?[1] In other words, what is it that relates determining and necessary processes to free, casual occurrences? To explain this, Althusser uses the concept of *overdetermination* borrowed from psychoanalysis. This concept alludes to the fact that changes—even if revolutionary—in the economic structure do not cancel the "survival" of all kinds of institutions and ideas that are "typical" of previous periods. He also makes a complementary reference to the process by means of which a new economic structure recreates and stimulates this kind of "survival." Clearly it is not merely a case of permanent contradictions being overcome or mediated by Hegelian means. The concept applies to the link between phenomena or segments considered "abnormal," "atypical" or "dysfunctional" and the "normal," "average" and "coherent" course of society. It also applies to what has been called unequal and combined development, immersed, nevertheless, in the global course of the dominant structure.[2]

It is interesting to note this issue of overdetermination was developed in the 20s—in a particular way and within a specific

1. L. Althusser, *Reading "Capital,"* London: NLB, 1977, p. 186.
2. See Althusser, *Pour Marx*, chapter 3.

medium—by Dashiell Hammett, one of America's most acute writers to gain insight into the secrets of capitalist society at the time. In his famous novel *The Maltese Falcon*, his protagonist, the detective Sam Spade, recounts a parable which has every right to be considered by Steven Marcus[3] as pivotal to Hammett's entire work.

I would like to pause at this point and expound upon as well as analyze this parable. The action takes place in the early 20s in Northeast America. The protagonist is a man named Flitcraft who, one day, having left his real-estate-office in Tacoma for luncheon, never returned. He failed to turn up to play golf after four that afternoon, although he had made an engagement to do so less than half an hour before going out for luncheon. His wife and children never saw him again.

Clearly, what we have here is an unusual event inscribed in the peaceful and mediocre life of a "typical" American citizen trapped in the "American way of life" structure. Investigations concerning the reasons for Flitcraft's sudden and strange disappearance help to complete the picture:

> His wife and he were supposed to be on the best of terms.
> He had two children, boys, one five and the other three. He
> owned his house in a Tacoma suburb, a new Packard, and the
> rest of the appurtenances of successful American living.
>
> He went like that, Spade said, like a first when you open
> your hand.

From the very outset, this story poses the problem of the unusual and abnormal event inscribed in the context of a process ordered according to the typical tendencies of society. Flitcraft's life harbors no specific contradiction that might explain his disappearance. His life simply reflects the contradictions of the entire American system. The detective's investigations—similar to social science studies—lead him to discover an explanation for this phenomenon.

> Well, that was in 1922. In 1927 I was with one of the big
> detective agencies in Seattle. Mrs. Flitcraft came in and told us

---

3. "Introduction" to D. Hammett, *The Continental Op*, New York: Vintage Books, 1975, p. xv.

somebody had seen a man in Spokane who looked a lot like her husband. I went over there. It was Flitcraft, all right. He had been living in Spokane for a couple of years as Charles—that was his first name—Pierce.

Here we have a clear philosophical reference, since the new name adopted by Flitcraft is none other than that of the founder of pragmatism, Charles S. Peirce (the two vowels have been inverted), whose ideas would prove fundamental in William James' elaboration of his own well-known proposals. Charles S. Peirce (1838–1914) sustained that truth and the meaning of ideas should be valued in terms of their practical consequences; from this he derived a curious series of speculations concerning change and love—according to him, the core of human development. In brief, this was the philosophy which derived from and suited the average man in American society at the time.

Hammett's version of this philosopher, a Flitcraft transformed into a Charles Pierce from Spokane, "had an automobile-business that was netting him twenty or twenty-five thousand a year, a wife, a baby son, owned his home in a Spokane suburb, and usually got away to play golf after four in the afternoon during the season." What happened? Simply that Flitcraft reproduced in Spokane the *very same* life he led in Tacoma.

> His second wife didn't look like the first, but they were more alike than they were different. You know, the kind of women that play fair games of golf and bridge and like new salad recipes.[4]

The problem Hammett poses here is that of the conditioning effect of the global social structure on its parts. The main issue is not the explanation of the behavior—based on external determinants (America's capitalist "economic basis")—of a Flitcraft-Pierce who pragmatically reproduces in Spokane the very same life from which he had escaped back in Tacoma. On the contrary, the issue is that in both situations a global and structural determination is in operation (of all first and last "instances," whether economic, political or psychological) and is having an effect on the behavior of particular and

---

4. Dashiell Hammett, *The Maltese Falcon*, New York: Vintage Books, 1972, chapter VII.

individual elements. Moreover, it is not the contradictions embodied in the typical American way of life that drive Flitcraft to flee from Tacoma and to reappear in Spokane. In defining his concept of *overdetermination*, Althusser has asserted that,

> it is important to fully understand that this mutual conditioning of "contradictions" does not cancel the dominant structure ruling over the contradictions and within them. . . . Quite on the contrary, the manifestation of this dominant structure is what constitutes, within the reality that conditions the very existence of each contradiction, the reality of the whole.[5]

The sun of overdetermination shines on us all.

Let us return, however, to our friend Flitcraft, whose adventures may perhaps provide a better explanation of the topic being discussed. So far, we have taken a look at what constitutes the *dédoublement* in Flitcraft's overdetermined life. Let us now take a look at what drove him to change the life he led for what would end up as exactly the same kind of life. The reasons for Flitcraft's flight are recounted by the detective Sam Spade:

> Here's what happened to him. Going to lunch he passed an office-building that was being put up—just the skeleton. A beam or something fell eight or ten stories down and smacked the sidewalk alongside him. It brushed pretty close to him, but didn't touch him, though a piece of the sidewalk was chipped off and flew up and hit his cheek. It only took a piece of skin off, but he still had the scar when I saw him. He rubbed it with his finger—well, affectionately—when he told me about it. He was scared stiff of course, he said, but he was more shocked than really frightened. He felt like somebody had taken the lid off and let him look at the works.

In a parody of Peirce's pragmatism, Hammett introduces chance as revealing the true "works" of life. Change does not intervene in this case as an expression of the necessary and determining process of Flitcraft's boring life; on the contrary, it attempts on the latter. The philosophical problem posed here is no longer concerned with the general totality and particular event relation, linked in a

5. *Pour Marx*, chapter 6.

content-form or essence-existence chain whereby one can interpret the fact that Flitcraft is trapped in an overdetermination that establishes a parallel between his life in Spokane and the one he led back in Tacoma. What we have here is the intrusion of an authentically undetermined fact attempting on the normal course.

> Flitcraft had been a good citizen and a good husband and father, not by any outer compulsion, but simply because he was a man who was most comfortable in step with his surroundings. He had been raised that way. The people he knew were like that. The life he knew was a clean orderly sane responsible affair. Now a falling beam had shown him that life was fundamentally none of these things. He, the good citizen-husband-father, could be wiped out between office and restaurant by the accident of a falling beam. He knew then that men died at haphazard like that, and lived only while blind chance spared them.

Our friend Flitcraft thus discovers he has lived trapped within a contradiction, in an absurd life. The dilemma emerging from Hammett's parable is which of these two is more fundamental in Flitcraft's life: his reabsorption into the network of overdetermining mechanisms, or the unsuspected presence of contradiction? Althusser would probably answer that since the presence of the totality of the invariant structure within contradiction proved to be over-determination, Flitcraft was overpredestinated to reproduce in Spokane the comfortable misery of his previous life. Let us proceed, though, with the parable, since Flitcraft's excursion towards Spokane was not uninterrupted:

> It was not, primarily, the injustice of it that disturbed him: he accepted that after the first shock. What disturbed him was the discovery that in sensibly ordering his affairs he had got out of step, and not into step, with life. He said he knew before he had gone twenty feet from the fallen beam that he would never know peace again until he had adjusted himself to this new glimpse of life. By the time he had eaten his luncheon he had found his means of adjustment. Life could be ended for him at random by a falling beam: he would change his life at random by simply going away. He loved his family, he said, as much as he supposed was usual, but he knew he was leaving

them adequately provided for, and his love for them was not of
the sort to make absence painful.

He went to Seattle that afternoon, Spade said, and from
there by boat to San Francisco. For a couple of years he wandered around and then drifted back to the Northwest, and
settled in Spokane and got married.

Hammett's fine sense of irony is worth noting here as he pokes
fun at the pragmatism espoused by Peirce and William James who
judged every idea according to the action that derived from it and in
function of the totality of its practical consequences. The irony lies
in that the pragmatic proposition is described by using the example
of a man concerned with establishing a coherence between his acts
and the essence of life, within the atrociously ordered context of
American middle class which, interrupted by chance, leads Flitcraft
to adapt to the unexpected in a highly conservative way. Despite
Hammett's mocking tone, he cannot conceal the bitter background
of a situation that offers no new alternative. Flitcraft

wasn't sorry for what he had done. It seemed reasonable
enough to him. I don't think he even knew he had settled back
naturally into the same groove he had jumped out of in Tacoma. But that's the part of it I always liked. He adjusted
himself to beams falling, and then no more of them fell, and
he adjusted himself to them not falling.

This is the dramatic story of a persistent overdetermination.
Although an element appears here which, regardless of Flitcraft's
capacity to adapt, escapes the actual concept of overdetermination,
namely, the *fact*—whether abnormal, hazardous or absurd—that
sometimes beams do fall and change the course of a man's life.
Unless we regard the fall of a beam as overdetermined by industrial
capitalist development and reflected both in urban growth and in
the need to demolish buildings so that cities may be remodelled.
Ugh!

The hazardous, unusual event in this parable symbolizes the
contradiction in which Flitcraft was inscribed; the mediating structure (or overdetermination) is so effective that it leads him to behave
aleatorily, like a vagabond—to adapt, in other words. Should we
seek a simile in history, his period of vagrancy could be compared to

a period of crisis during which profound social contradictions are revealed, although no social forces exist capable of finding a true alternative. That alternative appearing on the horizon is really no other than a second version of the *ancien régime.* Contradiction and its signs are thus taken prisoners and thrown into the fiery lake where mediating flames burn their subversive impulses.

The Flitcraft parable exemplifies the operation of a mediating structure capable of drowning profound contradictions. In a sort of mimetism, human behavior (vagrancy) is situated in concordance— apparent and illusory, although extraordinarily efficient—with the contradiction that suddenly emerges thanks to a chance event (the threat of death posed by a falling beam). The full conscious realization of the possibility that one could die any moment brings about a singular adaptation to the fact—which is probably all the more representative of this contradiction—of the extinction of life, the negation of life.

This curious adaptation becomes an aleatory action of escape, mediating the mediocrity of middle class life and the undeniable fact that contradicts it; namely, a senseless death. This is to say that the nonsensical reveals the contradiction of the social life in which Flitcraft is trapped. In fact, as we have seen, his life as a vagrant ended by being a mediation between Tacoma and Spokane. A bridge, in other words, not between two opposite poles, but between two variations of the same "American way of life," and therefore an illusion. Flitcraft's flight, however, did contain embryonically the elements of a radical revolt which, instead of ending as the Armageddon battle did, could have led to a total subversion of the conditions of life that engendered it.

xx The Resurrection of the Corpses

(Judgment)

The rest of the dead did not come to life until the thousand years were over.

Rev. 20:5

Nothing has stirred such deep theoretical repudiation among revolutionaries as the treatment of death, unless it is embellished by a heroic halo, as an extraordinary deed. Nevertheless, nobody can deny its overwhelming and anonymous presence. Inversely, the ruling classes have—and particularly in periods of crisis—inspired lengthy and baroque disquisitions on death; they have managed to cover this unique fact which is, indeed, the social and psychological event that admits the least mediation of all, with religious and philosophical gilding that seeks to keep the dead alive so the living may be deadened.

The anxiety produced by death has acquired a modern—or should we say Freudian—peculiarity with the development of the individualistic principles governing liberal bourgeois society. Could Locke or Bentham have ever imagined that the principles of liberal individualism would intensify anxiety regarding death's inevitability? The *Ego* of modern society is enshrouded by death defined in essence through exclusion; post-death and pre-birth empty spaces, for instance. It is no wonder that David Cooper points out the relationship between madness and the "places before our birth and after our death."[1] Madness is a rupture of the membranes separating the *Ego*—that is, the individual—from *the Other*, which is, ultimately, death, since it is precisely "the other" because the *Ego* is absent, and since death is recognized as the absence of the *Ego* perceived as a self-conscious individual particle.

The modern fear of death is inseparable from the individual's position as a fundamental juridical-political actor of the capitalist social contract. Edgar Morin has stated that death is at the root of

---

1. Cooper, however, having embarked on a search for new forms of transcendence, believes LSD, meditation or madness enable us to "experiment" these spaces. David Cooper, *The Grammar of Living*, London: Penguin Books, 1974.

individuality, although the individualist paroxysm increases the anxiety of death.[2] One could say that the treatment of death and of the dead in capitalist society is as important for the reproduction of the system as its counterpart, namely, the consolidation of individual rights. Capitalist society requires specific ceremonial forms to manipulate death, whereby it stimulates individualism without causing a generalized anxiety. Modern society seeks new ways of administering the natural phenomenon of the extinction of life insofar as traditional religion—together with its ancient funeral ceremonies—lose their effectiveness in a dual process where cosmetics endow death with apparent life and death is maintained in the world of the living.

Let us take a look, then, at some of these new forms: thanatopraxis and funeral homes. A rough description may give an idea of what these mean.

Thanatopraxis consists of a technique whereby a corpse undergoes somatic treatment and is then stored, a practice that substitutes the ancient religious one of simply burying mortal remains in a cemetery as soon as possible. By means of this treatment, certain animate characteristics are restored to the corpse to preserve it. The procedure consists of a thorough cleansing of the tissues by injecting the femoral, axillar and carotid arteries with a product containing formol, mercury, arsenic and lead. *Thanatyl*, as this liquid is called, functions as a blood substitute and contains dyes that pigment the tegument; it hydrates the corpse, giving it a healthy look and prevents the ocular cavities from sinking. A liter of *thanatyl* is enough for 154 pounds of corpse meat. Every cavity undergoes careful treatment. Viscera are punctured and their contents suctioned, eliminating gases, liquids and faecal material. A healthy, well-looked after corpse can last many months.

Sophisticated thanatopraxis can work marvels with corpses deformed by accidents, skin diseases, cancer and other mutilations. There are specialized treatments for overweight or pregnant corpses. In special cases, and with the aid of photographs, the thanatopractitioner is able to reconstruct the split image of the live body. In

2. E. Morin, *L'homme et la mort*, Paris: Seuil, 1970.

addition to the chemical treatments, makeup is used to conceal cadaverous lividness and the darkening induced by formol. Small operations, sutures, injections and prothesis help to correct the rictus of the mouth and the sinking of the eyelids.

A corpse can thus be conveniently mourned by his relatives and friends in ultramodern funeral homes, discreet places where preservation-reconstitution treatments are carried out to prevent the horrendous spectacle of putrefaction. Funeral homes (which the French euphemistically call *athanées*) lodge corpses in such a way that all ancient images of dirt and worms are effaced; they are placed on shelves or in wall-cavities, inside many-storied modern buildings with large, comfortable carpeted rooms where the body can be shown and mourned, rooms that provide seclusion for relatives visiting their dead. An American funeral home announces its services in this way: "For the dignity and the integrity of your deceased . . . A funeral home is not more expensive . . . Easy access. Private parking for a hundred cars." A funeral home project submitted in 1976 by a French architect about to obtain his degree, shows a true lay temple, "an appropriate place endowed with mediation and symbols that will make individual and social behavior easier in the face of death."[3]

What I have briefly described is not merely how commercialism and consumerism adapt to the field of dead body hygiene, nor is this only a modern form of dressing death with animate attributes to diminish distress for the living. Thomas is right when he says that the re-invention of mortuary behavior causes "the irruption of another form of the sacred," in which a "technical extreme unction" could be the beginning of a "lay ceremonial which, by its power of consolation, will make up for lost religion."[4]

Death undergoes therewith a true invasion of modern techniques and comfort. The process does not conceal death, however; instead, it re-introduces it under a new aspect within advanced modern society, since its elimination from daily life might provoke serious upheavals in basic mediating mechanisms nurturing the

---

3. D. Rochette, quoted by Louis-Vincent Thomas, *Mort et pouvoir*, Paris: Payot, 1978, p. 129. My description of thanatopraxis comes from this book.
4. *Ibid.*, pp. 130–31.

individualism required for the reproduction and accumulation of capital. The manipulation of death is similar to the imaginary engendering of marginal social spaces that serve to define normality; the concept of death with which civil society enshrouds the individual helps to define normality and homogeneity in terms of a consumer and wage-earner, as an atomized and exploited person commuting "freely" in capitalist market spheres.

(The World)

Then the One sitting on the throne spoke: "Now I am making the whole of creation new," he said.

Rev. 21:5

The essays contained in this book attempt to look into the relationship between the reproduction of modern political domination forms and the legitimacy endowed to them by certain current dualist and classificatory expressions of what is known as structuralism. I allude to those forms of thought—originating either in plain common sense or in exquisite intellectual sources—which advance with powerful analytical and dialectical weapons and cover an exuberant, contradictory and heterogeneous social life with the mantle of a network of cultural mediation. My main example has been the normal-abnormal dichotomy, since in one way or another —whether explicitly or implicitly—it has become one of the most outstanding expressions of classificatory and dualist thought. This image, that has its origins in pathology, has found its way into social sciences—frequently in a mathematical-statistical guise.

The procedure I have followed is to insert the essays within a game of imaginary networks and to build them around two models. The first is the Apocalypse, a literary work illustrating in the most terrifying way the damage caused in Western culture by dualist thought, an ideological nightmare plagued with political imagery synthesized in the war waged by the pagan mass of Babylon the Great and the chosen of New Jerusalem. The second model is the Tarot, a divinatory card-game based on Medieval classificatory imagery, a popular and rudimentary typology of human phenomena, still used nowadays to fill in the disquieting gaps that beset modern societies.

The plastic beauty of both the Apocalypse and the Tarot images has enabled me to extend this game—as an experiment—in Adela Trueta's 22 drawings that seek in their own way to synthesize the ideas discussed in each essay. It is up to the inquisitive and playful reader to seek for the intimate relation between the 22 essays, the 22 drawings, the 22 chapters in Apocalypse and the Tarot's 22 main arcana. I spent many a delightful hour in the company of Adela Trueta, when she was drawing the cards, and other friends became immersed in these speculations.

I have, nonetheless, devised a kind of index in which ideas expressed throughout are presented with the aim of providing the reader with a guide and, perhaps, eventually, show the link between them.

where. In pantheistic esoteric traditions, the idea of omnipresent power is linked to the assumption that god's name is in everything (cabalistic traditions and tetragram symbolism)......................p. 33

V. At their outset, small marginal and dissident sectors translate their perception of an omnipresent oppression into apocalyptic visions. The moral authority of those revealing the end of a period or predicting the end of the world is overwhelming. This creates a kind of dogmatic social priesthood, in which benevolent and meek preachers are ruled by a pontiff who establishes himself as the expression of normal and commonplace feelings. p. 43

VI. The way marginal phenomena—whether embodied in individuals, groups or ideas—operate within society resembles vaccines; they are false enemies unleashing limited and relatively harmless wars that end by strengthening the health of the social body (normality). Many marginal sects express the impotence underlying their struggle by organizing family-based unifying forms that seek to reconstruct a religious variety of pristine love as an antidote to the contradictions ensconced in modern bourgeois life.........................p. 55

VII. Limited wars weave a dense mediating network—full of signs, symbols, ideas, myths and characters—that encloses society and is governed by entirely different rules from those of State apparatuses and the mechanisms of traditional political hegemony. These mediating networks, like chariots riding to war, are permanently in motion even when their aim is immobility; their movement seeks to protect the permanence and immutability of society as a whole......................p. 69

VIII. Certain modern political theories based on the fact that the relationship between new marginal sectors and society provide non-democratic forms of stability, state the necessity of institutionalizing and legitimizing these processes as theatrical forms of political dynamics, thereby substituting the ungovernable trends of current democracies. The struggle is legitimized and organized with such equilibrium that not even a struggle takes place, but, rather, an equivalent exchange of signs and signals that substitute a violent exchange of action. . . . . . .p. 79

IX. The objective conditions of the new political processes of legitimization in the new State are given functions that extend considerably into mass organization of peripheral not strictly capitalist conditions of the productive process. The vast sector of dependent bureaucrats, technocrats, intellectuals, employees and petty bourgeois engendered in relation to the State (the so-called "middle class") is the best breeding ground for declassment and social mobility processes. It is here that singular forms of *embourgeoisement* and proletarianization at the root of the growth of non-democratic mediation and legitimizing structures are produced. In this context, Diogenes would tire of seeking with his lamp the man bearing the revolution. . . . . .p. 89

X. Mediation networks of capitalist societies grow essentially from the articulation points between structures that contain their own dynamics and automatism—such as private enterprises and the capitalist market—and structures engendered by external factors, such as State actions. The dynamics of the former imply their own process of extinction, curbed by the latter kind of structures which have extended considerably forming the so-called Welfare State. It is difficult to determine exactly to what extent chance is trapped in the closed logic of this system or whether, on the contrary, its regularity is devoured by the game of chance. . . . . .p. 101

XI. Various socialist and Marxist trends have upheld that the possibility of reaching a truly democratic socialism is only feasible in developed capitalist countries where the State has acquired wide social functions, which means it need not be destroyed in a revolutionary process. The main setback of such interpretations is they ignore that the new forms of State in advanced or late capitalism constitute extraordinarily powerful non-democratic legitimizing forms of exploitation. The new force that seems capable of dominating State violence could become a far more subtle stabilizing power. . . . . .p. 107

XXII Epilogue: The Imaginary Networks

(The Fool)

"These others must stay outside: dogs, fortune-tellers, and fornicators, and murderers, and idolaters, and everyone of false speech and false life."

Rev. 22:15

No sooner does the universe of modern bourgeois exploitation close its circle of immanence and coherence than the blurred image emerges of those who are imaginarily evicted from society become the enemies and destroyers of the dominating system. Simultaneously, however, the system's imaginary networks enmesh the evicted enemies once more, compelling them to act out a simulacrum. This enactment occurs because the modern State is closer to a *space* than to an instrument of domination. Moreover, it organizes political relations in terms of space, not merely controlling the class struggle, but *occupying* it and allowing itself to be *occupied* by it. If we take this as our starting point, the nature of the imaginary networks of political power becomes comprehensible. Sartre discovered long ago the relationship between spatial concepts and the illusions of immanence which he stated:

> Without even realizing it, we think that the image *was* in the consciousness and that the purpose of the image was *in* the image. We imagined consciousness as a place inhabited by small simulacra which were the images themselves. Undoubtedly, the origin of this illusion must be sought in our habit of thinking within space and in terms of space. We shall call it the illusion of immanence.[1]

We now know, moreover, that insertion into spaces is more than a habit; it is one of the ways in which the State manifests itself in daily life. We also know that imaginary simulacra are a constitutive part of political power. I therefore find it interesting to conceive the modern State as a looking-glass, that is, a combination of spaces: real and imaginary, material and reflected.

One must steer clear, however, of the typical temptation of

1. Jean Paul Sartre, *L'imaginaire: Psychologie phénoménologique de l'imagination*, Paris: Gallimard, 1940, p. 15.

linear Marxism of interpreting imaginary networks solely as the external illusory solution of real contradictions, high up in the clouds of mythology, religion and real contradictions.[2] The mediating networks of imagination are present in the actual constitution of exploitation relationships, not merely in terms of a deceptive fetish concealing contradictions but as an illusory element essential to the actual development of contradiction, exploitation and antagonism. Social relations and the products of labor—alluded to by Marx in his study on the law of value—thus transformed into phantasmagoric forms and hieroglyphics do not merely have a concealing function that turns antagonistic contradictions opaque; antagonism could not, in fact, exist if it were not imaginarily expressed.

This same set of imaginary networks also shows that, despite everything, the entirety of the social movement is not previously inscribed in and confined to the immanent structure, waiting to be deciphered. Society is obstructed by wavering and erratic lines that escape all logic; what they reveal is that great revolutionary explosions as well as minor daily life dramas are not wholly trapped by the unrelenting rationality of the social structure, awaiting a hypothetical liberating crisis that will rend illusive wrappings. On the contrary, there actually does exist a disorder at the very heart of social facts that is linked within the determining structures of society.

POSTSCRIPTUM

When I wrote this book at the end of the seventies, disorder had penetrated structuralist and Marxist explanations. It was moreover obvious that the legitimacy of scientific knowledge and modern political systems was on the threshold of a crisis. We are still experiencing the aftermath of this crisis which adopted a spectacular mien in 1989 with the velvet revolutions, a term coined by Havel regarding the changes in central and eastern Europe. This disruption dissolved the great structures and—with the end of the Berlin Wall—brought to an end a world divided into two immense political-military blocks that faced each other. The study of imaginary networks explores the new alternatives offered to our fin de siècle culture by seeking to avoid interpretations which regard men

---

2. See Cornelius Castoriadis, *L'institution imaginaire de la société*, Paris: Seuil, 1975.

as mere ghostly props for overwhelming structures and blocks; this exploration also seeks to avoid, however, the opposite extreme of considering social activity as a summary of an individual behavior oriented by rational aims. As I see it, the imaginary networks are not determined by the disappearance of subjects by the weight of immanent structures, nor can they be explained by the transcendent hyper-expansion of actors whose rational behavior lights up the chance spontaneity of social conglomerates. The imaginary networks are neither omnipresent structures that explain social behavior, nor illusory images originated by the conscious activity of individuals. They refer to the coexistence of incoherent deed and consistent structure, to the simultaneousness of chance and reason, to the cohabitation of spontaneity and determination or, voiced in traditional terms, to the presence of freedom and necessity in history. Viewed from this perspective, many social contradictions and political paradoxes are not overcome nor do they reach a synthesis, but remain unresolved for lengthy historical periods.

We have been—and still are—facing a global crisis concerning legitimacy: that which emerges from the discourse and that which sustains the political system, that which illustrates ideologies and that which stimulates criticism. Both the revolution and the establishment lose legitimacy, as do egalitarian utopias and liberal hierarchies. In the name of what or whom do we resist, lend our support, protest, criticize or explain? The disillusionment that emerges from this crisis of legitimacy now has a name: *postmodernism.* Every page of this book is overwhelmed by that curious melancholic pessimism that characterizes what Lyotard has called the postmodern condition. Nonetheless, these essays seek to touch rock bottom concerning the very problem that motivates their pessimistic throbs: that of legitimacy. As creatures of the legitimacy crisis, we are doomed to commence time and time again our explanations regarding the future of society and the meaning of history.

One of the central ideas I use as a starting point for understanding the legitimacy problem of modern political systems can be outlined as follows: there is a close relationship between, on one hand, the tendencies towards declassment and displacement (metaphorically referred to in the book as the *embourgeoisement* of the proletariat and the proletarianization of the bourgeoisie) and, on the other, the imaginary networks that engender normality and marginality myths. Both the development and application of this idea have laid bare the cohabitation of radically different social planes that, resembling topological spaces with reflecting mirror-like surfaces, intercross in a crazed ritual dance in which the order of movement and the disorder of gestures mysteriously coexist. Social classes are a good example of these mirroring topological spaces; as I see it, the "class struggle" cannot be understood as a dialectical process which will sooner or later—and by means of a Hegelian series of mediations and transcendences—reach a synthesis that will erase contradictions and differences. On the contrary, we are now faced with a situation in which both poles remain essentially different and irreducible and, though they may evolve, they can never merge together in a spiral of overcomings; polarity is extinguished before any dialectical mediation can take place. The same can be said of other planes and spaces, such as that examined at length in this book, of the marginals and normals, those imaginary symbols and real actors of chaos and order. Traditionally, social science has found it difficult to accept the simultaneous presence of chaos and order in a lengthy coexistence that shows no indication of being resolved or overcome by dialectical mediation. The imaginary networks provide, so far as I can see, a concept capable of accounting for this basic heterogeneity; these networks conceal differences and contradictions even as they show the irreducibility of many cracks intercrossing the social body. Although during my research I used Marxist lenses, the latter were mounted with an optic that had its starting point in the principle of the essential heterogeneity and fragmentation of society. In this sense, the optical observation apparatus comes closer to a kaleidoscope than to a microscope.

An important aspect of this optic lies in the focus of the kaleidoscope on liminal regions, on those fringes of transition and those borderlines where *different* spaces or periods touch or come close together. If society is a fragmented and broken soil, it is worth looking into the interstices to investigate what is going on there. Since the crack is an incurable wound, how can societies reach cohesion and unity during lengthy periods of time? What is the nature of the mediating crevice, if mediation is impossible? Although I had, at the end of the seventies, no prophetic intentions when I pointed

the kaleidoscope of my wishes towards those liminal zones—
namely, socialist countries—a critical panorama emerged, predicting its imminent collapse. I simultaneously pointed out that what
some analysts defined as a crisis of the advanced capitalist State was
in fact a renewal of legitimacy forms which might endorse postdemocratic forms in western countries. My impression is that both
in socialist and capitalist countries these imaginary networks of political power have operated in the same way and have generated—
despite the vast difference in socio-economical textures—similar legitimizing effects. Nevertheless, Gorbachev's *perestroika*—as well as
its spectacular effects in the 1989 central and eastern Europe revolutions—show that socialist societies are reaching a limit beyond
which they are incapable of reproducing the authoritarian mechanisms of domination that proved to be their hallmark for several
decennia. The question is—why?

It seems to me that an important part of the explanation can be
found in the particular evolution of the mediating spaces in socialist
countries. This evolution had trapped all legitimizing and mediating instances (such as mass media, ideologies, science, art, education, health service institutions, religions, national cultures) within
the sanctuaries of a gigantic and oppressive State. There the mediation structures grew tremendously, to the extent they became an
immense center of disruption that contaminated the whole; critical
and democratic tendencies grew at random within the State tower,
invaded each and every pore, contributing to undermine inefficient
central planning mechanisms. In this way, a State which should
have administered itself with utmost rigor and the blind automatism typical of police mechanisms, discovered within its bowels the
growth of an increasing mass of functions it was unable to digest.
The State was growing and at the same time something inside clam-
ored for its extinction or radical transformation.

What endorsed the slow putrefaction of the socialist State was
not so much the personal character of the dictatorship (that of Stalin,
Brezhnev), as what could be called *autocracy*, defined in its strictly
etymological sense of a government capable of automatic self-repro-
duction and self-sufficiency. The *autarchy* of political life contra-
dicted an economic life lacking in autonomy, that was subjected to
the political will. The result was paradoxical: predictable politics

and unpredictable economy. In this amazing inversion lies the root of the socialist regime deadlock and putrefaction. In Marxist terms, one could say that politics in socialist countries are the hard structural basis of society, whereas economy grows in the superstructural branches. Political autarchy—and its blind machine-like nature—ended by crushing the very legitimizing functions it had seized. To this was added the increasing inefficiency of a centralized economy subjected to the rhythms of a political apparatus that was becoming increasingly irrational, precariously shielded by a vast parallel and clandestine black market. Socialist economy, in its different variations, has sought in vain to transform social equality into a price-fixing mechanism to avoid engendering political unbalance; it is here that the permanent contradiction between plan and market emerges.[3] I sometimes think that the inversions and transpositions observed at different social planes—such as those that alter economical and political roles in socialism—are similar to these processes of sensorial substitution—generated by the use of prothesis—which have enabled neurologists to explore cerebral plasticity and thereby open up new perspectives for mental function research. When politics substitute economy, we may imagine that the governing apparatus becomes an immense living prothesis, whereby new means restore the legitimizing sensibility of the system, and mediating networks are thus created within spaces that were fulfilling other functions.[4]

I am aware that in this book I have inverted traditional ideas on authoritarianism in socialist States; it is usually politics that seem a strange world, opaque, and unpredictable, to many "Kremlinologists." On the contrary, economy appears to be severely controlled by strict central plans and watched over not only by bureaucrats but also by the KGB police and the army. Now, after the 1989 collapse of European socialism, my idea that so-called real socialism is by nature entirely different to anything known in the western capitalist world has been confirmed, together with the fact that the notion of

---

3. See Michael Voslensky's book *Nomenklatura*, Berlin: Verlag Fritz Molden, 1980, particularly chapter IV, a good analysis of the economic irrationality curbing the development of USSR technology.
4. This idea came to me during conversations with my friend Paul Bach-y-Rita. See his book *Brain Mechanisms in Sensory Substitution*, New York and London: Academic Press, 1972.

totalitarianism can do nothing to help us understand the hidden tendencies of this new form of domination.[5] We now know that under the mysterious opacity of socialist country politics there was nothing more than a drab struggle at the pinnacle of the ruling party. We also know that behind the five-year monolithical plans, a strange socio-economic life was concealed, whose peculiarities were never reflected in the grey and deceiving statistics. The impossibility of establishing self-regulating mechanisms within the economy induced the monstrous growth of all kinds of bureaucratic and administrative processes—very often contradictory among each other—located at every level and in every channel of the system of production and distribution. This amazing baroque entanglement of controls and decision-taking instances sired the expansion of an economic space which not only ended by being inefficient and backward, but also engendered unpredictable and unexpected effects. One of these is the strange transition towards capitalism which is making its way thanks to *perestroika* and the 1989 velvet revolutions. However, this is not a conservative process that will produce social and economic regression; as a system, socialism established in the 20th century has proved to be incompatible with democracy, so that in these conditions any democratic reform usually comes hand in hand with a move towards a market economy. In this very context, the market has become an advanced element; time will have to go by before those nations that have undergone an authoritarian socialist period can experience the painful conflict between mercantile logic and the vitality of representative democratic spaces.

These facts, together with others, have shown that socialist society, far from being a unified total space, occupied by an immanent power in a totalitarian way, is conformed by an ill-assorted group of differing and contrasting planes. The unifying and totalizing mantle is in fact an imaginary network that conceals and legitimizes the new forms of exploitation and domination. I do not in the least wish to mollify my reflection on the nature of real socialism by erasing the label of *totalitarianism*. It does seem to me, though, that

5. Edgar Morin's essay, *De la nature de l'U.R.S.S.*, Paris: Fayard, 1983, is a good example of the confused conclusions that are reached when the USSR is regarded as a totalitarian society. According to Morin, the only hope for change in the Soviet Union was the advent of a military dictatorship.

by placing the totalitarian label on these forms we cloud over those mechanisms that not only legitimize socialist States but also provoke profound tendencies leading to change and collapse. The similarities between Soviet socialism and fascism are insufficient for both experiences to be assimilated in a single model, and the risk entailed is that of spreading the idea that nations ruled by communist parties can only move towards democracy by means of war. This political logic has informed western post-war governments and nurtured a cold war that has curbed renovating tendencies in socialist countries. Fortunately these tendencies, summoned by Gorbachev, have managed to emerge before military confrontations could hinder reforms and endanger mankind.[6] The powerful imaginary networks that entangled Soviet society have begun to fray and disintegrate.

While I was writing this postscriptum, another dramatic manifestation of the imaginary networks of political power broke out, a terrible effect of that unquenchable thirst of legitimacy of the modern States that continues to engender spectacular wars. This time, however, the imaginary ingredient brings with it an alarming dose of military destruction and violence. The United States, as a means of reaffirming its hegemony after the wreck of socialist power, has begun a large-scale war against Iraq in the Persian Gulf; once the great traditional enemy—Communism—has crumbled down, there now emerges the evil figure of a muslim dictator, Saddam Hussein, embodying all the dangers of a wilderness that threatens Western civilization from the very depths of the desert. The apocalyptic symbolism—used throughout the book—seems highly appropriate for describing the end of the millennium watermarked by the war in the

---

6. We must recognize in Khrushchev an important precedent as regards the curbing of authoritarian and militarist tendencies engendered by socialism itself. We should remember that in 1962 Commander Fidel Castro formally proposed that, if Cuba were to be invaded, the USSR should wipe out the USA by delivering the first blow in a nuclear war. "It would be," he stated, "an act of the most legitimate defense, however hard and terrible the solution, because there is no other." Khrushchev's answer was: "In your cable dated October 27 you propose we be the first to deliver the nuclear blow against enemy territory. Of course you understand where that would lead to. It would not merely be a blow, but the beginning of a thermonuclear world war. Dear comrade Fidel Castro, your proposal seems mistaken, although I understand your reasons." (Cabled letters October 27–30, 1962, revealed by Castro himself by means of the French writer Jean Edern Hallier, published in *Le Monde*, November 24, 1990.

Persian Gulf and scourged by the "desert storm," as American strategists call it. Indeed, we are witnessing the dreadful spectacle of the Chosen of New Jerusalem bombarding the pagan masses of Babylonia. The fact the war should actually occur in the geographic space occupied by Babylonia long ago merely adds another sinister tinge to the déjà vu of this war. It is as if the depths of the Western collective unconscious were being bombarded so as to destroy the monsters created by the delirium of industrial and technological civilization.

The banality of the reasons for this war merely underlines the horrors of capitalist liberal utopia which—far from bringing peace and quiet—initiates its recently recovered world hegemony with a genocidal war against Iraq. The defense of Kuwait's oil reserves and of the borderlines imposed by colonial domination does not conceal the perverse western impulse which has aggravated and stimulated a poor and marginal minor dictator such as Saddam Hussein, turning him into a terrible enemy who embodies all the evils of terrorism, of religious fanaticism and fascism and of the third world otherness. It is true that as soon as the capitalist world closed the circle of its own immanence, there emerged the specter of the imaginarily expelled pariahs who represented—on a planet scale—the Jezebel syndrome previously analyzed in this book; a wrathful oriental Jezebel who rebels against an imperialist Captain Ahab who is still unable to control the white Leviathan. The near East and North Africa have become, day by day, the great breeding ground for the real and imaginary enemies populating western nightmares. Before President Saddam Hussein, the menacing figures of Colonel Muammar al-Qaddafi and the Ayatollah Rihollah Khomeini had emerged. The bestiary created by western nightmares also includes, quite obviously, Uganda's General Idi Amin Dada and Panama's General Manuel Antonio Noriega, surrounded by a colorful aura both real and imaginary, that has nurtured the racism of the silent majority world wide.

The U.S. war against Iraq, the end of the second millennium's watermark, has a sense of the déjà vu to it not only because it seems to come straight from the Bible and seems predicted by a magician reading the Tarot to President George Bush. This war has already occurred time after time in popular imagery and in literature: it has been created by the imaginary networks of political power. Millions of children throughout the modern world have read in comics or watched on TV those epic encounters enacted by the silent majority superheroes, wielding highly sophisticated weapons, using ultra-modern electronic technology and upholding crass morals. The marginal antiheroes are eccentric criminals and fanatic third world militaries who use traditional and cruel forms of combat. In brief, Washington's computers versus Baghdad's poisonous gases; Bush's artificial intelligence versus Hussein's natural cunning; western air-sea technology versus trenches teeming with oriental barbarians; the factory versus the anthill. It would seem that symbolic structures were being reproduced as if they were real political and military effects; as if strict military logic derived from the irrational delirium of the imagination.

This war—a thousand times imagined, dreamt, wished for—has broken out at last. All the historical and religious imagination of the West is now concentrated in the Mesopotamian desert, staging by means of a great battle a sinister flashback that sums up two millenniums of wars. All the demons of the West crowd around in Baghdad, at night when the bombs fall, to dance a sinister witches' sabbath. The western world—as if in a Freudian oneiric delirium—has displaced and condensed in the near East all the conflicts, unsatisfied desires, anguishes and failures that torment it, in such a way that the war against Iraq is both the dream and the nightmare of a world painfully journeying towards a new order. This war is the immense mediating apparatus where the correlation of forces between Europe, the Soviet Union, Japan and the United States is being decided by means of blood and gore. The new world order is being melted and molded in the sands of the desert, far away from any civilized metropolis, so that the majority of the victims will not bloody Europe's soil, as occurred in the previous two World Wars. How many more wars must be borne in this transition?

Relatively limited wars—such as those of Iraq, Korea, Vietnam—can also be regarded as shows in which the imaginary networks that lend legitimacy and meaning to the new postdemocratic political forms in the West are being woven. Thus, to parody a happily coined expression of Pierre Bourdieu, I could say that these

spectacular wars are *needed* without being *necessary*.[7] This is exactly
what happens to the imaginary networks: they engender effects
which are needed but not necessary. Society casts its imaginary networks because it needs to catch the slippery fish of legitimacy, which
it frequently does manage to catch, in fact. But it is obvious that the
fish is not *necessary* for the network to be woven. This particular
link—which is not one of determination nor the outcome of a rational action—situates us in fertile theoretical soil. A lofty point
from which we can peruse the historical horizon and contemplate the
great spectacle of the imaginary networks woven by the war. As I
have said before, the spectacle occurs in liminal areas where no dialectical synthesis is in operation, where there are only transpositions
and intrusions of actors and symbols unknown to each other; their
spectacular confrontation engenders an aura that is visible and comprehensible from many different and even opposite points. The very
contemplation of the spectacle creates an effect of legitimacy precisely because in it there appear heterogeneous signals given by the
Other, by another period, another culture, another religion, another
world. It suddenly seems that, thanks to the spectacle, mediation
and communication are achieved (it remains unknown whether it is
thanks to or despite of the disasters caused by the war); it seems that
the actors which move and are moved by the imaginary networks
understand each other. These networks, however, are not means of
communication but a means of legitimizing, of creating differences,
division and domination. Plurality is the constitutive form of social
reality, even though it may borrow the mask of unity and may wear
a military and militant uniform. A dormant plurality engenders
uniformity monsters, but when it wakes up, the threads become
entangled once more, and the particular color, texture and language
of each thread become manifest. In war as in peace, communication
or mediation is impossible, although nothing is to prevent the inter-
woven social threads from forming a network and representing a
spectacle. Do the actors in a play understand each other? The fact
they cannot do so and that they can only recognize the cue for their
entrance and for saying their lines in no way undermines the meaning of the spectacle. The actors are similar to the fish in that they are

7. "Fieldwork in Philosophy" in *Choses dites*, Paris: Minuit, 1987.

unnecessary as regards the weaving of the network that catches them.

Similarly, we cannot cease to interpret social changes or peruse the future. Do we communicate with the future? Are we determined by the glimpse we manage to catch? Do we understand what is to come? We do not know, but we still belong to a period in which men cannot stop themselves from looking into the distance, towards where the arrow of time points. We are still living in Dante's *Inferno*, the inhabitants of which explain to the poet that *You may understand, therefore, that all our knowledge shall be a dead thing from that moment on when the door of the future is shut.*

Mexico, February 1991

Index